LIFE

David Sutch was bo[...] in 1940. As Screaming Lord Sutch he became a leading light of the '60s pop scene with his group the Raving Savages, who still regularly perform all over the country. He first stood for Parliament in 1963 in John Profumo's ex-constituency and created the extraordinarily popular and seminal Official Monster Raving Loony Party. Now featured in the Guinness Book of Records as having stood a record number of times in a Parliamentary by-election, he and his party are now an instantly recognizable and much-quoted part of the British political scene.

Peter Chippindale, co-author, is a former *Guardian* journalist and now a full-time writer living in north Cornwall. He is author and co-author of *Stick it Up Your Punter!*, acclaimed by *The Times* in 1990 as 'the funniest book of the year, if not the decade', *Disaster! The Rise and Fall of News on Sunday, British Monarchy plc*, and, in 1991, *Dished!*

ALSO BY PETER CHIPPINDALE

Disaster! The Rise and Fall of News on Sunday
Stick it Up Your Punter!
British Monarchy plc
Dished!

Life as Sutch

*The Official Autobiography of
a Monster Raving Loony*

Lord David Sutch

WITH PETER CHIPPINDALE

Fontana

An Imprint of HarperCollinsPublishers

Fontana
An Imprint of HarperCollins*Publishers*,
77–85 Fulham Palace Road,
Hammersmith, London W6 8JB

Published by Fontana 1992
1 3 5 7 9 10 8 6 4 2

First published by
HarperCollins*Publishers* 1991

The Authors assert the moral right to
be identified as the authors of this work

ISBN 0 00 637805 6

Set in Linotron Palatino

Printed in Great Britain by
HarperCollinsManufacturing Glasgow

CONTENTS

for my mother,
Annie Emily Sutch

'There's no success like failure,
and failure's no success at all'

BOB DYLAN

ACKNOWLEDGEMENTS

We both owe a debt of gratitude to a large number of musicians, Loonies, and alternative thinkers who over the years have contributed ideas and thoughts which have surfaced in this book. More specifically thanks go to Alan and Norma Hope for both help and access to the OMRLP archives, Pauline Healy, Trevor Priske, Sally Crawford for her help with the manuscript, David Hughes and everyone at EMI for re-releasing my *Screaming Lord Sutch Story* album, and Giselle for her patience. Peter Chippindale would also like to thank his old partner, Chris Horrie, for a few lines borrowed.

This book was put together at various locations and on that front we are indebted to Ros and everyone at the Golden Lion, Ashburton; Ursula at the Bistingo, Old Compton Street, Soho (site of the old Two I's coffee bar); the staff at Napoleon's, Openshawe, Manchester; Tony and Val King and the kids in Skelmersdale, Lancashire; and Phillip and Brenda Harrison in Wraysbury, Berkshire.

Many thanks also to Thann and Stan, Tristan Lord Sutch, (Uncle) Reg Calvert, the legendary Joe Meek, Tom Littlewood, Jan Clayton, Alan Clayson, Graham Cole, Pat and Ken Hellier, Russell Newmark, Barry Collings, Ritchie Blackmore, Jimmy Page, Jeff Beck, Mike and Babs Delaney, Arthur Martin, Bob Geldof,

Dave Dix, Gloria Walker, Dick Knowles, Paul Barrett, Dave (Batman) Goddard, Ron Long, Chris Gatting and the Undertakers, all the Savages, Rapiers, Jaguars and Sunsets, Steve Golly, Glen Stoner, my councillors Freddy Zapp, Charlie Salt, Alan Hope and Richard Vero, Valerie Bird, Kim Roberts, Ronnie, Denise and Bell Kellerman, Big Del Richardson, John Ward, Keith Hunt, Johnny Rogan, Ken Rumens, Top Hat Owen, Stan Hurley, Peter Stringfellow and Sir John Mills, Graham Sharpe and Tim Moss and all at William Hill, Riaz Dooley king of the bucket shops, International Press Cutting Bureau and David Bailey.

Above all we would like to acknowledge the support and guidance of our agents, Mark Lucas and Cat Ledger, and our editor, Val Hudson.

Thanks, too, to No. 10 Downing Street for providing the backdrop to the front cover photograph, and to John Wallace for taking it.

BORN TO LOSE

IT WILL not surprise close observers of the political scene, or anyone who has met me, that it was Winston Churchill who set me on the road to becoming Britain's most successful politician.

Like many others of my generation, I will always be grateful to Churchill simply for making such a good job of the Second World War. Thanks to him from my earliest days I was able to experience the horrors and deprivations of armed conflict at first hand. But in addition Winston also handed me a special, personal legacy which has shaped not just my own life, but the political life of the country.

I was in every sense a war baby, conceived almost at the instant Churchill was taking over the reins of the War Cabinet from Neville Chamberlain. The coincidence in the timing of the two events was significant. But unlike the then Greatest Living Englishman, who had Chatsworth House to play with, I was born into humble circumstances. Not for me the silver spoon, the rolling acres, the comfortable family seat waiting to be inherited. Rather, I was fated to begin life as a mere grain of the salt of the earth in the more mundane setting of North London.

My mother, Annie, had come down to London from a pit village near Sheffield at the age of eighteen, and met my father, William, who lived in Cricklewood.

Naturally, he knew Lloyd George. They were married shortly after war broke out, managing a brief honeymoon during the 'phony war' before hostilities began in earnest.

Again significantly, I was conceived just as Churchill was taking over the reins of the War Cabinet from Chamberlain, and born in New End Hospital, Hampstead, on 10 November 1940. By then Dunkirk had been and gone, the Battle of Britain had been fought in the blue skies over Kent, and London was buckling down to the grim realities of Hitler's Blitz.

Heartbreak Hotel

If I had been old enough to focus, I could have been misled about my background by my first home – an enormous mansion stuffed with treasures off 'millionaires' row' – in the Bishop's Avenue in Hampstead. But in reality the house belonged to the Sokoloffs, a family of Russian Jews who had been evacuated to America. My parents were only living there because they were the caretakers.

Mr Sokoloff himself had remained in England and moved into a flat in the West End. But he visited the house regularly, bringing with him famous names from showbusiness and boxing, including the promoter Jack Solomons and the music hall artist Wee Georgie Wood, whose knee I sat on.

The big house was a grand and comfortable place to be, up the hill out of central London and therefore comparatively safe from the bombing. We were very settled there, and it seemed we had been blessed with at least a touch of life Upstairs until, when I was only nine months old, tragedy struck our little family. My father, who I never got to know, had enrolled as a War Reserve policeman and died serving his country. Riding to Hampstead police station on his motorcycle in the blackout, he failed to notice a concrete air-raid shelter sticking out into the road as its red warning light had gone out. He rode headlong into it and was killed instantly.

Within weeks my widowed mother and I were told we had to vacate our luxurious surroundings.

Mamma Mia

When she had first come to London my mother had gone into service with a solicitor's family in Cricklewood. After they read in the paper about my father's death they contacted her, offering us both a home for life, saying they would semi-adopt me and make sure I got good schooling. It was a difficult decision for Mum, as she had no income apart from a small pension from my father. Rooms were hard to get when you had a young child and when she went to the Welfare, all they could suggest was putting me in a home.

But despite the generosity of the offer, my mother dreaded the thought of spending her life trapped in a large house looking after three children and doing the housework and cooking. Instead she thought about getting out of London with all its dangers and returning to her roots in the Yorkshire pit village of Woodhouse. Her father had been a miner until he was gassed at the Somme and both he and his wife were still alive. But their cottage was tiny and they already had a Bevin boy, a lad who had to work in the mines instead of doing military service, staying with them – I believe that this was the village in which Sir Jimmy Savile was also once a Bevin boy. The issue was decided when my mother's sister, who also had a young child and whose husband had been taken prisoner at Dunkirk, went back to my grandparents' cottage instead.

I will always admire Mum for sticking it out on her own the way she did. She was a great fan of Charles Dickens, and had named me David after David Copperfield. Like Mr Micawber, she always believed something would turn up and, on this occasion, it did when an elderly couple she knew offered her the spare bedroom in their house in Glengall Road, Kilburn. In return Mum had to do domestic help for no pay, but at least we had a roof over our heads, although as we were in the top room she had to drag the pram and everything else up at least fifty stairs.

But the couple were good to us, and they must have asked their friends for clothes for me, as we never had to buy any. To supplement my father's pension Mum found work at British Home Stores in the High Street, only a few minutes away. This suited her well as she always preferred working in cafés and shops to being stuck inside a house because she got to meet people.

The arrangement in Glengall Road worked well for a time, but the house was very cramped, and when I was three we had another offer and moved to a house in the next street, Charteris Road. We were to stay there for the next twelve years.

Sugar Shack

Charteris Road was a dead-end street of terraced houses and we had the upstairs flat, sharing the bathroom and also the garden, in which the woman below kept chickens. We were lucky in that she was stone deaf, so she didn't mind me rampaging around as I grew up.

The woman herself had had a lucky escape when the factory where she worked had received a direct hit. She looked up from her bench actually to see the bomb explode, but miraculously was unhurt. Everybody else had run for the shelter when the siren sounded but, being deaf, she had never heard it.

Our two rooms were unfurnished, so Mum and I made a series of trips to Chapel Market in Islington where she painstakingly collected bits and pieces of cheap furniture and the pots and pans we needed. You always hear talk about the wartime spirit and the way people helped each other, but really there were probably as many sharks – or spivs as they were called then – as there are today.

I remember one time when Mum bought a square of oilskin from someone selling at the doorstep to brighten up the flat. Disastrously, the pattern came off the first time she washed it, and it turned out not to be oilskin at all, but painted cardboard. After that she never bought at the door again!

Life was hard in many ways. When I was given my first banana I thought it was a toy gun, and didn't realize I could eat it. Another famous flop in our lives occurred when Mum queued for three hours for two oranges, only to find afterwards one of them had dried out. I now live near the Portobello Road and I am always reminded of that incident when I so often see oranges which have been carelessly thrown away lying in the gutter.

People have since told me politics is always jam yesterday and jam tomorrow but never jam today. On that score I didn't have a political upbringing – as far as I was concerned as a child there just wasn't any jam at all.

There were kindnesses from our relatives in Yorkshire, such as one memorable Christmas when my grandfather sent us a chicken. Unfortunately all we got delivered was the box. I solemnly explained that the bird must have got homesick and flown back to the country!

But the dingy surroundings of our street were alleviated by a small park close by, and at the weekends Mum would try to compensate by taking me to roam round Hampstead Heath and on special treats to the river at Richmond or Kew Gardens.

Eve of Destruction

By the time we moved to Charteris Road I was old enough to get a place in the government day nursery in Neasden and my mother would drop me off there every day before going on to do war work at the Smith's clock factory up the road.

Some of my earliest memories are of standing in the freezing darkness waiting for the morning bus. Our area was badly hit by the German bombing and after a raid you would witness the extensive damage. I clearly recall being enormously impressed by seeing some dummies which had been blown out of a shop window and strewn across the road like a ghastly collection of naked bodies.

On other occasions you would see people calmly eating their breakfast with their windows gone after the night's raids, torn curtains flapping in the wind. My gran in Yorkshire made me a lovely little siren suit like the one Winston Churchill wore, but trimmed with leopardskin fabric, which I proudly wore when my mother took me down to the local park. This park had a barrage balloon floating above it, and it was full every evening of people getting some fresh air before gathering up their bedding to spend the night in the tube station to shelter from the bombing which would start when darkness fell.

But although we lived opposite the entrance to Kilburn Park tube, we never once took refuge either there or in an air-raid shelter. My mother would not even go into the cellar of the house as – although she never admitted it – I think she was afraid of being buried alive. But we were lucky as although houses either side of us were bombed we never had so much as a broken window. We would sit in the flat listening to the terrifying noise of the bombs falling, or alternatively, from when I was very young, Mum would take me to the cinemas and music halls a short bus ride away at Marble Arch. When the air-raid sirens sounded a sign would go up on stage advising us we could go to the shelters, but we used to stay put as, in the best showbiz tradition, the show always went on. These performances were a wonderful example of the best of the wartime spirit, but for me they were overshadowed by the greatest show of all: a private viewing that took place one morning at the end of Charteris Road.

When I was a child I was often accused of having more imagination than was good for me, and it's only because I still have the scar to show for it that I can be certain of what happened on that fateful day.

Hit Me With Your Rhythm Stick

Ever since I could remember, the voice of Winston Churchill had boomed through our house on the radio. I had grown up literally in our Leader's shadow, and even when I was a babe in arms Mum had comforted me by declaiming the speeches with which he rallied the nation in its darkest hour. Some of my earliest memories are of seeing Churchill driving through the streets of Kilburn. He struck me as a terrifying, imposing figure, sweeping by in a gigantic shiny black car, reclining in the back with his ever-present cigar.

Most days, preoccupied with the more important matter of despatching the Hun, he ignored small people like me on the pavement. But one momentous day, when the war clouds were rolling away, Jerry was on the run, and victory was soon to be ours, the car stopped for him to take a brief walkabout amongst his people.

The chauffeur opened the back door, and to my huge excitement the Great Man stepped out in all his fine clothes, wearing his trademark, a Homburg hat. As he walked down the street supporting himself with his stick, I hurried to kneel before him. To my eternal joy, he spoke to me.

'Who the hell are you, and what's your name?' he bellowed at me, prodding me with the cane.

Young though I was, I summoned up the courage

to reply. 'My name's David,' I said shyly. 'David Sutch.'

'Sutch! Sutch! What sort of name is that, eh?' he barked back. 'Come on, boy! Speak up!'

I saw his brow clouding over and I remember how petrified I was as he leant over me and stuck his great bulbous face next to mine. I found myself enveloped in a cloud of acrid cigar smoke which made my tender eyes water. 'I was named as Sutch, and I'm just a little one, sir.'

'Just a little Sutch, eh?' he mused, pausing for a moment as he patted me almost fondly on the head and looked deep into my eyes. 'Well, Sutch, such it shall be then,' he went on, giving me his famous V for Victory sign. 'For Sutch is the way it is; and Sutch is therefore the way it will be when I am gone.'

Then his mood abruptly changed and he suddenly scowled at me like a British bulldog, whose nature he shared. 'Now, Sutch, get out of my way, you little squirt!' he shouted, and as he did so he took his fat cigar from his mouth and stubbed it out on my outstretched, pleading hand. As I recoiled, shrieking with pain, I did not immediately grasp the significance of the incident. All I knew was that my hand hurt like hell. It was only later that the truth dawned. The hand the Greatest Living Englishman had scarred so badly was my voting hand.

By that branding he had passed on the torch of his destiny, and that of the British people, to little me.

MONSTER MASH

AFTER THE war life improved for everyone. At the top of the political tree, Winston was replaced by a Labour government under Clem Attlee which started erecting the Welfare State to make things better for people in humble circumstances like us. And for kids like me in the crowded inner city things really looked up. We had the bomb sites as prototype adventure playgrounds and now that the blackout was lifted we stopped spending all the hours of darkness tripping over kerbs. For the first time in my life we could show a light through the window without an officious air-raid warden yelling at us to turn it off. During the war we had been lectured that even a lighted match could be seen miles away and would make us a target.

In reality it was the beginning of many grey years of post-war austerity and there was still strict rationing. But, never having known anything better, we children were happy as we queued for our first taste of little luxuries, such as ice cream. And at last we could throw away the hated cardboard boxes containing our gas masks which we had always had to carry on our backs like a snail's shell.

For Mum and I life took a dramatic upturn when she met a manfriend with a car who took us out on trips. Once the barbed wire had been removed from the beaches we had already been on day coach trips to resorts like Brighton, Southend and Margate and now we went further – even on two momentous occasions to Cornwall and across the sea to the Channel Islands.

Once, when we were at Southend, Mum had her first intimation of something which is still with me today. I got separated from her and ended up in the lost children's tent, which I thought was great as I was given lemonade and biscuits. But my complete lack of a sense of direction remains and even though I can travel hundreds of miles touring without any difficulty, I still get lost in parts of central London I should know like the back of my hand.

Puppet on a String

After the war as a child I would often spend long holidays with my mother's family in Yorkshire. After my cramped life in the upstairs flat in Kilburn the wide open spaces up north were a revelation to me. There were lots of other children in the village for me to go exploring with, and I experienced many things for the first time. I saw allotments, played with whippets, and began my lifelong fascination with street markets. It was with my gran that this obsession was first triggered off when she took me to the open market in Sheffield and I was in thrall to the atmosphere.

But Gran changed my life even more by buying me some hand puppets which I took back to London. During my trips to the seaside I had always been entranced by the Punch and Judy and Pierrot shows on the beach and at the end of the pier, hanging around their tents endlessly rather than building sandcastles like other children. Now, back in Charteris Road, I started entertaining my friends with the hand puppets on the pavement outside the house. Seeing this, a neighbour wrote to the *Kilburn Times* which printed a story. A woman then called to ask me to entertain at her son's birthday party and Mum gave permission but refused a fee, saying that giving the show would be treat enough for me. She was right. I was regally transported there and back in a car and had the thrill of giving my first show to an indoor audience.

My growing interest in entertaining was further fuelled by an uncle in Yorkshire who took me to Butlin's at Clacton, where I hero-worshipped the Redcoats. And it was here, at the age of twelve, I gave my first stage performance, singing 'How Much is That Doggie in the Window?' My prize was a clockwork mouse, which I then used to torment mercilessly the girls at school.

Mary from the Dairy

All through my childhood Mum continued to take me to the music hall and the variety acts. The greatest of these was at the Metropolitan in Edgware Road where the two-hour show cost two shillings. It was composed of twelve acts which were a real mixed bag, ranging from singers and comics to fire-eaters, magicians and trick cyclists – I got plenty of grazed knees trying to emulate them on my bike at home! I was particularly enthralled by performers like Wilson, Keppel and Betty, who did a mixed act including their famous sand dance, the Harmonica Gang and comedians like Max Wall.

But most of all I was influenced by Max Miller. He

will always be the Number One for me – the best stand-up comic of all time. I was dazzled by his flash suits, which were like silk curtains decorated with huge flowers and rainbows, and his walking stick with diamonds sparkling in its handle, which he told the audience had cost £2000 – a lifetime's money for people like us.

Somehow I instinctively understood his knack was all in the timing, and I was mesmerized by the hypnotic power he had over his audience and the way he made everyone laugh with his relaxed and easy chat. He always started his show by telling the audience he had two books of jokes – a red one and a blue one, and which would they like? They always chose the blue jokes, of course, and I loved them even though I was so young I only understood about one in five of them. But that didn't stop me trying them out on others, and Mum would cringe as I endlessly repeated one of my favourites in the greengrocer's by holding up a potato and saying: 'Look – King Edward's!' Even though I did not get the joke myself, what I did know was that it made people laugh.

I was just as fascinated by our many visits to the cinema, where I'd sit for hours with Mum watching flickering black and white films. I was also a devotee of the Saturday morning children's matinee at the nearby Gaumont State Cinema on Kilburn High Road, which claimed to be the biggest cinema in the world. I would wait impatiently all week to see the next round in the adventures of characters like the Three Stooges and Dick Barton, Special Agent.

But the film which made the biggest impression on me was *Treasure Island*. It was from watching this that I first learnt the meaning of the expression 'to jump out of your skin' during the scene where Blind Pugh grabs the boy, Jim Hawkins, in the darkness. Of course the other kids and I all identified with Jim and we spent endless hours playing 'pirates' on the bomb sites. I was too young to be allowed to see anything very strong, but I still found myself irresistibly drawn to anything slightly spooky or with horror in it – a fascination fuelled by visits to Madame Tussaud's and the Tower of London.

I was eight when I fully graduated from the hand puppets Gran had given me to Punch and Judy. I knew instinctively this old puppet show summed up the vocation Winston Churchill had thrust upon me, and I realized later in life that the crocodile and the ghost said everything there was to know about politics – frighten them first and if that doesn't work then give them lots of stick.

Of course I was too poor to buy a Punch and Judy in a shop, so I resolved to make my own. In those far-off days, before DIY superstores and MDF chipboard, wood was a scarce and valued commodity and I had to scour the bomb sites to obtain the supplies I needed. I was as happy as a sandboy whittling away with my penknife, when I saw an extraordinary thing was happening. The Punch I was carving was turning into the spitting image of Winston Churchill! When I showed it to my childhood friends they just laughed, believing I was no good at carving, but I later recognized it was yet another sign of the destiny guiding my scarred hand.

School's Out

As a grain of the salt of the earth, I did not go to Harrow School like Winston, or indeed to anywhere special. Instead it was at the local state school in Salusbury Road that I learnt more about my Mentor and the rolling tide of history of which he was but the latest wave. But I had other lessons in life to learn at school, such as wheeling and dealing in Batman and Dan Dare comics. And as there was no school debating society for me to demonstrate my emerging talents, my juvenile skills were forged more in the rough and tumble of the playground.

I was a schoolboy swimming champion before switching to boxing, which was more useful to me as I was small and therefore likely to be picked on. I wanted to be like my hero, the world heavyweight champion Rocky Marciano, little realizing I was destined to end up as a short-arse. But at my own featherweight I still did well, becoming first Kilburn and Willesden, and then Middlesex, schoolboy champion.

Academically I was not a distinguished child, but that did not stop me having correct intimations of my coming greatness. I remember the headmaster once calling me into his study and sneeringly asking me: 'Well, Sutch, what are you going to be when you grow up?'

With all the heady confidence of youth and an instinctive sense of my role in history, I replied: 'One day, sir, I intend to be Prime Minister and rule the country.' How he laughed as he smote me with his ruler and chased me from the room. But would he still be laughing if he was with us today, I wonder?

Waterloo

Naturally, the subject of history fascinated me and I studied the greatest and most consummate leaders of the past with the object of taking a leaf out of their book. I learnt about the tricks of the world's great politicians – Lenin, Stalin, Bismarck and the British giants Peel, Disraeli, Gladstone with his bag, Lloyd George, and all the kings and queens who had ruled before them. Harold's really getting one in the eye at Hastings showed me the necessity of always being on the look-out; Henry VIII taught me the importance of wine, women and song, and certain historical episodes really caught my imagination.

My friends and I made Roman chariots out of orange boxes, and matching wooden helmets with brushes screwed on the top, and then fought as gladiators with wooden swords and squares of garden netting. Endless spiders were sacrificed for my Robert the Bruce impersonation, and how Mum laughed when I attached kitchen knives to the wheels of my tricycle to imitate Queen Boadicea's chariot and slashed the legs of the kitchen chairs to ribbons! Then I burnt the cakes like King Alfred, and there was the even more hilarious episode when I re-enacted the Defenestration of Prague with the neighbour's cat!

But the historical role which most interested me was that of the court jester. The jester seemed to me to be more on the line than the king. A king could be quite unready like Ethelred; stupidly try to hold back the sea like Canute; or simply be insane like George III, yet it didn't seem to matter. But if you were a jester, and your jests were no good, they had your head. You found yourself literally dead for what you said.

As juvenile political activity I stood for election as a prefect, beating other boys bigger than myself and confirming another lesson from history – you don't have to be big to be a winner. I added Napoleon to my list of heroes, and like him found I enjoyed dressing up in silly clothes covered in gold braid, topped off with a tricorn hat.

Funnily, my worst subject was music. I was always bottom of the class and got slung out of the choir for singing offkey, whilst attempts to get me to learn the recorder were abandoned in despair.

Go, Go, Go, Little Queenie

In June 1953 I sat down on my plastic commemorative cushion in pouring rain outside the DER showroom to watch the Coronation on TV. This was the year I became a teenager – old enough to know the new Elizabethan Age had dawned, but too young to appreciate its significance.

At our street party that day I nonetheless resolved that when I came to run the country there would be a Coronation every week. Unconsciously I had already picked up on the bread and circuses importance of the Royal Family as entertainment – a message which at that stage the press had yet to grasp.

It was as I left school, three years after Queen Elizabeth's enthronement, that Mum and I finally escaped from Kilburn to South Harrow, where we moved into our first real flat. It was over a shop in a pleasant area, and the change after our grimy,

busy street life in downtown Kilburn was enormous.
By moving I also forged another link with Winston, as
we were within walking distance of the famous school
where he had been taught. I would regularly visit this
imposing building, rubbing my toes along the worn
stones of the steps and imagining the sharp clatter of
his leather soles as he went into the dusty classrooms to
absorb the knowledge he would one day use to rescue
the nation.

So just as we moved to Harrow and Winston's successor Sir Anthony Eden was ploughing his political
career over Suez, I left school to start my working life.
Like so many of the kids I knew I had little choice and
just because I had been good at metalwork I was sent
to a sheet metal factory off Hanger Lane in Willesden.
On my first day I was shown round the filthy, noisy
building and solemnly informed if I stayed there for
the rest of my working life I would get a good pension
at the end of the day. There and then I decided I would
rather starve than waste my life like that and walked
out. Instead I tried other jobs, like being a plumber's
apprentice and working as a 'spanner boy' for a garage
mechanic, as I was interested in cars. But I was soon
bored with the everyday grind and tedium and having
so little to show for it at the end of every week.

Like so many of my generation I felt imprisoned in
a dreary past and turned to music for consolation. In
those days we teenagers rejected the tyranny of the
fuddy-duddy old BBC, which had nothing for us,
and instead huddled under the bedclothes to tune
our radios and home-made crystal sets to the hidden
delights of Radio Luxemburg.

One night I was listening to old Dickie Valentine
crooning on about the Sandman when WHOP! –

suddenly a new sound blasted out which was like nothing I'd ever heard before: 'One, two, three o'clock, four o'clock, rock! . . .' Bill Haley and the Comets had arrived and my world, and that of all my friends, changed for ever. There was even more excitement when the film of *Rock Around the Clock* arrived in Britain and played to packed cinemas. But what we fans were all really waiting for was the chance to see this wild rocker Bill Haley in the flesh.

See You Later, Alligator

There was a curious delay between us first hearing those opening words of 'Rock Around the Clock' and Haley crossing the Atlantic, which I only understood later. In 1956 he and the Comets had more success in the British charts than anyone before, but the fans had not yet grasped that, far from being every teenage girl's dream, Haley was a fat, middle-aged man by our standards. He was thirty years old and had been married twice. And if we thought that was ancient, one of the co-writers of 'Rock Around the Clock', Max Freedman, had been born in 1893!

As his record company had rightly feared, when Haley did eventually appear in Britain the fans sent up a universal groan of disappointment – all except for me. For I saw instantly this wide-faced, chubby man, old and pasty-faced though he was, bore a striking resemblance to the man who had handed me my destiny. Apart from the kiss-curl, which was obviously a cunning attempt at a disguise, Haley was the spitting image of Winston Churchill! And, I realized with even more excitement, there was a very good reason for this – Churchill's mother had been American!

Here, I saw, was the next sign on the road to my destiny. The Winston legacy had found its direction in my new-found passion for the music of rock and roll. It was my fate to be one of the lead voices of the new generation which was rising up from Tin Pan Alley on the historic mission of sweeping away the world of the old fogeys for ever.

'I know it's only rock and roll, but I like it,' I thought to myself and millions of other teenagers were thinking the same thing. Who now thinks of the politicians of that period, such as Patrick Gordon Walker or George Wigg? Instead the names forever inscribed in the hall of fame are ones like Bee Bumble and the Stingers, Johnny and the Hurricanes, and above all the great giants of rock and roll – Jerry Lee Lewis, Little Richard, Chuck Berry and the King himself, Elvis Presley.

There and then I resolved to be a rock and roll singer. And as the first step towards my aim I relocated myself to the exotic setting of the Cannibal Pot coffee bar on the Harrow Road in Wembley.

Tell Laura I Love Her

The Cannibal Pot was the local hang-out patronized by bike boys and Hell's Angels and as I went there on my newly acquired second-hand BSA Bantam 125cc I was the pits. The bike scene in those days was very hairy, with big Triumphs, Nortons and 1000cc Vincents, and I was made to join in the races based round the famous Ace café on the North Circular Road.

At the Ace there was an evening event in which each

biker put a £1 note on the table, and a record was put on the jukebox. As soon as it started everybody ran for their bikes and roared down the road, round the roundabout, and back into the café. You had to get back before the record finished and the fastest not only scooped the pot, which was often more than a week's wages, but also got the pick of the birds.

This event would be followed by another race from the Ace to the Busy Bee in Watford, with the police lying in wait for the unwary. It was dangerous madness, especially after it had been raining and the roads were slippery, and a number of the bikers were killed or injured. I had no choice but to join in on my Bantam or risk being rejected as chicken, but I soon found myself pressed into the role of passenger on a bike with a sidecar, which was even more frightening than being on two wheels.

The rest of the time the bikers just used to hang around the Cannibal Pot feeding the jukebox all day and welcoming anybody like me who contributed a few pennies. Alex, the burly owner, used to give us about three hours per coffee before we had to buy something. It was like a poker game in which you bluffed it out to the last minute and if you left it too long he would physically throw you out. Alex also amazed us by being a paid-up member of the Communist party which, rather than us not buying coffees, we put forward as the reason for his being so strange and aggressive.

When I'm Cleaning Windows

One day in the Cannibal Pot I met Big Ginger Bill, a huge youth resembling an American football player, who persuaded me to buy his window-cleaning round. For a payment of £15 I got a bit of rag and a tiny, tattered address book with lists of streets and numbers, all marked '2/-' and '3/ 6d' with every here and there '7/ 6d', which indicated a shop window which was the cream. With the book came a little wooden cart Ginger Bill had made himself to carry the ladder, which was equipped with a chain so you could hook it to the back of a motorbike and pull it along.

I found the window-cleaning round suited me perfectly. I could work the hours I wanted and, if it was freezing cold or raining, I could stay in bed and catch up later when the weather was better. Most of all the work gave me the freedom to be myself, let my hair grow long, and wear whatever I liked, as well as practise songs like 'Splish, Splash, I Was Having a Bath' as I went on my rounds. After the long hours spent draped over the Cannibal Pot jukebox I knew the words of all my favourites off by heart.

There were always plenty of cups of tea and the odd leg-over, which was embarrassing when you didn't get paid at the time and had to go back on Saturday morning to collect the money from the old man. I used to grin as I explained it was for cleaning the windows and then giving a quick rub-down with a chammy.

Meanwhile I could carry on with the serious business of hanging out in the Cannibal Pot and I was going on about how I was determined to be a rock star when one of the bikers suggested I went for an audition at the Two I's coffee bar in Soho.

Screaming Lord Sutch's Twenty Favourites

1 Colour – blue
2 Drink – tea
3 Food – jellied eels/French bread/ice cream/steak
4 Town – London
5 Country – America
6 Occupation – feeding the birds
7 Singer – Little Richard/Chuck Berry
8 Band – Credence Clearwater Revival
9 Guitar Player – Jimmy Page/Ritchie Blackmore/Jeff Beck
10 Film – *Citizen Kane/Treasure Island*
11 Actor – James Cagney/Humphrey Bogart
12 Book – *Animal Farm*
13 TV Programme – The News/The Brian Walden Interview/Fawlty Towers
14 TV Personality – Arthur Daley
15 Time – 1 p.m.
16 Car – Cadillac '59 (Super III)
17 Sport – boxing
18 Boxer – Rocky Marciano
19 Animal – Jack Russell terrier
20 Hobby – collecting junk and records

Rock with the Caveman

By now I was eighteen, the year was 1959, and the Two I's, in Old Compton Street, was already the legendary basement where most of the big British stars like Cliff Richard, Tommy Steele, Adam Faith and Paul Raven (later to become Gary Glitter) were discovered. One of its great legends is that Lionel Bart, who later wrote a string of hit musicals including *Oliver!*, once whitewashed the whole place in return for a meal as he was so hungry.

I made my way to this hall of rock and roll fame in deep awe and arrived to find myself in a long line of Elvis look-alikes, all holding their guitars and adjusting their quiffs. The basement was stiflingly hot and I almost choked on the Brylcreem fumes pouring off the row of DA (duck's arse) haircuts lined up in front of me. It was just beginning to occur to me that we all looked exactly the same when the guy running the auditions, who'd obviously had a trying day, shouted he was fed up. We could all shove off and come back the next day with something different, he roared.

'No more "Blue Suede Shoes", "Jailhouse Rocks" or "Heartbreak Hotels"!' we heard him yelling as we shuffled off up the stairs and back on to the street.

On my way home I got off the bus and was thinking about this when I passed Jack's second-hand shop. I always gave it a glance as a matter of course, but this time there, in the window, was a pair of buffalo horns. This gave me an idea, so I bought them for a couple of shillings. When I got back home I glued them on to the crash-helmet I wore for zooming about on the Bantam. Then I went scouting around for something to go with this headgear and my aunt offered me her leopardskin coat. I promptly improved it by tearing off the sleeves and the next day, nervously equipped in my new gear, went back to the Two I's to join the line of Elvis look-alikes who had turned up again despite the shouted instructions of the previous day.

That was the first appearance of my Wild Man of

Borneo look, designed to be deliberately raunchy and shake the grannies up by showing I didn't give a fuck. I wanted to be brash, exciting and hit everyone like a thunderbolt, so when it was my turn to be auditioned I jumped around, screamed, yelled, kicked and farted as I belted out an obscure old number called 'Bullshit Boogie'. It worked, and I was offered a spot on the spot.

The only snag was that my aunt did not share my elation. When she saw the leopardskin coat she was horrified and told me she had not been giving it to me, but only lending it. Now it was in tatters she demanded I pay her back. So, the result was that all the money from my first two gigs, at the Park Royal Hotel on Hanger Lane the Clay Pigeon at Eastcote nearby, went in paying off my debt. And despite what the auditioner at the Two I's had said, I always ended up doing 'Blue Suede Shoes' and 'Heartbreak Hotel' whenever I played the place because the backing band didn't know anything else.

But for me the Two I's was simply a launching pad for something much more radical.

Twist and Shout

To begin with my claim to fame was being the first of the long-hairs. Thanks to the freedom given to me by my window-cleaning round I had grown my locks to eighteen inches long and turned myself into a freak years before the hippies came along and screwed it up for me. In the days before the drug culture long hair was simply associated with rebellion and layabouts. People used to get very angry and shout at you in the street to get it cut and that you should be put in the army, so I decided to use it as the foundation for the outrageous act I had started constructing.

As I had grown up, my fascination with horror and the macabre had increased and I had spent many hours in the cinemas watching the great old stars like Boris Karloff, Bela Lugosi, and Lon Chaney, graduating to films like *The Mummy, The Phantom of the Opera, The Hunchback of Notre Dame,* and *Frankenstein.* More and more intrigued by the special effects I had seen, I now fused them with my Wild Man of Borneo stuff to create the new concept of 'rock'n'horror'.

Then I started putting a band together which I called the Raving Savages. It began one day when a tough-looking person walked into the Cannibal Pot and introduced himself as Carlo Little, telling me he had just come out of the army where he had been a drummer. I then recruited a young guy called Bernie Watson, who worked in the record shop up the road, as lead guitar; Rick Brown as the bassist; and as pianist Nicky Hopkins, who went on from me to back big-name bands including the Who, the Kinks, Rod Stewart, the Rolling Stones, Jefferson Airplane and Simon and Garfunkel.

We started practising in Slim Motors, a bombsite second-hand car dealer's next to the Cannibal Pot. But Slim soon decided we were a hazard to his trade, and to get rid of us paid for us to move up along another door to the Swan pub, where we rehearsed in a back room.

A young guy called Keith Moon lived along the road with his parents and idolized Carlo, who gave him lessons at 10/- a time in how to play two bass drums at once, which was the big thing at the time.

Keith would then come along to my gigs and take over halfway through the set to finish off the night. Thanks to my spots at the Two I's I soon got gigs all over London, enabling me to build my rock'n'horror act to its full potential. I based it on songs I wrote myself – 'Jack the Ripper', 'My Big Black Coffin', and 'All Black and Hairy' – and it was completely outrageous by any standards. In those more conventional days it caused an absolute sensation.

My Ding-a-Ling

The act started with the compere announcing the Raving Savages and the curtain opening to reveal only the gear, but no people, on stage. Then, to huge screams from the back of the hall, the band would run through the audience wearing nothing but leopardskin Tarzan leotards, making everyone jump. They would kick straight into a raunchy instrumental of 'Lucille', starting to march backwards and forwards as they gradually switched into the Death March. At this point four monks, led by Igor the bald-headed 'Mad Monk' bearing aloft a four-branch candelabra, carried a coffin in through the audience and placed it upright onstage.

I was in the coffin and Igor would slip in a mike so I could start screaming and yelling to a sound-effects tape of weird noises before launching into my opening number of 'Big Black Coffin'. I would poke big rubber horror hands out of the coffin lid as I sang before I leapt out to attack the girls in the first row. I was a nasty sight, my face covered with thick horror make-up of unearthly white, with black and red round the eyes to make me look as though I'd just been dug up. I would be wearing the classic horror gear of a dress jacket with the stuffing coming out of it, a black coat with a silk maroon lining and a top hat. To round off the effect I had a mouthful of green gunge which I spat over the audience. The halls were always so packed that the girls couldn't get away and I would bend down and run the rubbery hands over their faces and hair to get them screaming. They had already been excited enough by seeing the handsome guys in the band wearing nothing but leotards, and things would now really start to get going.

It began with smoke flares and flashing lights – there were no strobes in those days – and my grabbing a huge wooden club and crushing a few tin cans to warm things up. Then I started chasing the Mad Monk round the stage, swopping the wooden club for a rubber one behind the coffin where the audience couldn't see the switch. Re-emerging, I would whack Igor over the head as he broke a blood capsule to simulate his skull being split open and his 'brain', which was really a sponge, fell out of his hair. Then, to the accompaniment of wailing guitars, I would strangle him to death in front of their eyes.

To put the whole thing right over the top, the most handsome member of the band would then go to the front of the stage, skimpily dressed in his leopardskin leotard, and waggle his hips to make his parts joggle about. Whilst he concentrated the audience's attention I would stealthily go back to the coffin and reach in, where the audience couldn't see, to a bucketful of maggots. I'd get a good handful, creep up to the front, and then lean over and quickly stuff them down the front of as many girls' dresses as I could reach. At this they would go into hysterics, piss themselves, pass out, or do all three in quick succession. For an encore I would do the same trick again, but using a different bucket containing garden worms, some of which I always tried to get from the cemetery. The people at the back would be waiting for those upfront to get it again, but this time I would fling the worms their way. Some of them would always get enmeshed in the girls' beehive hairdos, sparking off a fresh shockwave of revulsion and panic.

The music then faded out on ''Til the Following Night', as I retreated back into the coffin, slowly pulling the lid down as the stage was blacked out.

I'd Like To Teach the World to Sing

I'd re-emerge for a series of straight rock and roll evergreens. I'll be the first to admit I'm not the world's greatest singer, but I am a good rock and roll shouter, which is a very different matter. A great ballad singer like Frank Sinatra has a voice that is just too good for rock; in fact there are very few artists who can do both – notably, in my opinion, Roy Orbison, Elvis Presley and John Lennon. For people like me the numbers which work best are the good belters which I used as my standards, like 'Roll Over Beethoven', 'Johnny B. Goode', 'Whole Lotta Shakin' Goin' On', 'Jenny Jenny', 'Keep A-Knocking', 'Long Tall Sally', 'Sweet Little Sixteen', 'Blue Suede Shoes', 'Tutti Frutti', 'Good Golly Miss Molly', and 'Hound Dog'.

I would do one or two straight, with just mild special effects like whirling the microphone stand round my head, but on most of them I included more elaborate theatrical effects. For 'Great Balls of Fire' I had a big black cooking pot on stage filled with rolled-up newspapers soaked in sump oil, with a dash of petrol to spice up the conflagration. I would chuck a match in after singing 'Goodness, gracious . . .' and when it flared up lean over and flick my long hair in and out of the leaping flames. For 'Splish, Splash, I Was Having a Bath' I stripped to a swimming costume and got into a tin bath with loads of bubbles. For 'Sweet Little Sixteen' I wore a pair of plastic tits, and I had a special cage to get into for 'Jailhouse Rock'. I danced with a medical skeleton for 'Bony Moronie'; dragged on a stuffed alligator to accompany 'See You Later, Alligator'; and put on a pig mask to sing 'Hog for You, Baby', as well as hanging a pink plastic toilet seat round my neck before eventually hurling it into the audience. Interestingly, this seemed to be regarded as the most outlandish of all the things I did and people would discuss it endlessly.

I called the whole act 'rock and roll vaudeville' and to my great satisfaction there seemed to be universal agreement it was the ultimate in bad taste and quite disgusting. The result, naturally, was that a lot of people wanted to see it – even if in some cases they ended up too stunned to applaud and just sat there gobsmacked.

Rip It Up

Most gross of all was the number which was the climax of the set – my own composition of 'Jack the Ripper'. I took the part of the Ripper by wearing a black top hat and a Sherlock Holmes cloak in evil-looking dark purple. With me I carried a Gladstone bag containing the tools of my wicked trade – a massive syringe, knives, scalpels and cut-throat razors. White opera gloves rounded off the ghoulish effect. The number started with a girl in tarty gear running across the stage panting with fright, to the accompaniment of an eerie Hammond organ-type guitar solo. Then I burst on and chased after her, lunging with a knife, which I twanged though the speakers so the audience would know it was real. I caught the girl in the middle of the stage and plunged the knife into her breasts whilst she let out bloodcurdling screams. After I had given her a good stabbing I dragged her over to a table where I ripped her open in a mock operation, dragging out a plastic heart and lungs which I'd dipped in water beforehand to make them look dripping and authentic. To boost the bad-taste factor I always gave these a quick lick before placing them in a silver kidney bowl I'd bought in the Portobello Road street market.

The next sequence would be heralded by a police whistle and a policeman dashing on stage. We would have a sword fight, first with my dagger, then moving up to cutlasses, and finally a huge Excalibur-type sword with which I chased him off stage. All that part was real pantomime stuff which I'd picked up from the music halls. The song ended with a last verse in which I produced a severed head with guts and bits hanging from it, which I would lean forward and wave in the faces of the girls at the front to make them scream even louder.

If I was doing a big show I'd go to the slaughterhouse in Harrow and buy pigs' hearts, lungs and heads, which I whirled round and round before sending them sailing into the auditorium. That always sent them running for the exits like rabbits. There were a few other stand-bys, like a guy with built-up shoulders and a false head, who carried a sauce bottle we'd nicked from a Wimpy under his arm and squirted it upwards as the false head was knocked off with an axe. Basically it was blood and gore everywhere.

Light My Fire

Of course such an over-the-top act was bound to run into trouble, even if it was over minor matters like during the Irish tour when they got things muddled up and we arrived to see posters plastered everywhere advertising 'Screaming Lord Sutch and the Raving Sausages'.

But the cutlasses and sabres were real and sliced fingers were regular occurrences. At the Golden Lion in Fulham I even broke a member of the audience's nose with the axe, and was lucky in his being quite happy to settle for a quick gin and tonic as compensation.

Other things were simple mistakes – like the time the monks placed the coffin the wrong way up, so I was upside-down and choking to death, and when the lid was eventually opened I fell out legs first. Once at the Sheffield Granada I was 'strangling' the pianist, Freddy 'Fingers' Lee, on top of his piano when it started rolling off the stage. With a terrified Freddy still clinging to it, it crashed into the orchestra pit below in a massive cloud of dust. He was lucky to be taken off to hospital with only minor injuries. The audience of course loved it and there was huge disappointment when I went up there again a few weeks later and the same thing didn't happen again.

The biggest danger was fire. I had a long pole with a branding iron on the end which I put in the firepot and then waved round my head and out over the heads of the crowd. Now and again it would catch a girl's dress and burn a big hole in it. Quite often the firepot itself would flare up and spill over, but I would be half-ready for that and could incorporate it in the act by my rushing off in a supposed panic to come back in a fireman's outfit with a watering can and bell.

But that part didn't always work and there were regular fires, like the one at the church hall at the Hayes End social club run by Father Gamm, a trendy American priest who later built a huge outdoor stage round the back and held the country's first pop concert, featuring Gerry and the Pacemakers and Del Shannon. The local paper, seizing its chance, headlined its report on my accident 'HOLY SMOKE'.

My Latest Flame

But the worst trouble usually came when I was beaten to solving the problem myself by a jobsworth in charge of the stage, who would pick up a fire extinguisher and cover the whole place in foam as if he had never heard of a fireproof blanket in his life. At the Star Club in Hamburg, where they couldn't understand what I was saying, the jobsworth lowered the curtain, and when that caught light the real fire brigade had to be called and I was nearly sent home.

The fireman routine had its own problems, like the time I threw the watering can into the audience at a DJs' convention in Hounslow and somebody threw it back, knocking over the firepot and starting a blaze which destroyed half the gear including the entire drum kit. Another time at the Southall community centre the brass bell flew off its handle and knocked me out, but as usual the crowd loved it, thinking it was all part of the act. The loudest cheers were for the real ambulancemen who came to take me away, for once covered in genuine blood.

But the real wild card was not so much the jobs-worths as the wallies. Half-drunken idiots would regularly leap on stage to 'save' the girl and have to be dragged off by the bouncers. The worst time was one heart-stopping moment when I was in full cry and a guy came rushing through the audience, waving a piece of paper and mouthing urgently at me. Because of all the drama I was convinced there must have been some major disaster and reluctantly waved the band to a stop before I leant forward to catch his words.

''Ere, can I have your autograph, please?' the wally asked, holding up what I could now see was not a piece of paper, but his stupid book for signatures.

Other people would come up at the end and moan it was in bad taste and they hadn't expected what they'd got, to which I had a simple answer: if they paid to see a band called Screaming Lord Sutch and his Raving Savages, I would tell them, what did they expect – Vera Lynn?

TALKIN' 'BOUT
MY G-G-GENERATION

BY 1961 MY act was fully established and I was a personality and a star. I set the seal on my success by going on the Granada All-Stars tour, with Mike and Bernie Winters as comperes wearing teddy boy suits, Gene Vincent, Mark Wynter, and Johnny Duncan and the Blue Grass Boys, who had had a smash hit with 'Last Train to San Fernando'.

Life was going well, and I had ditched the Bantam for a hearse which I used to drive around for my act. I also bought a metallic blue Chevrolet Impala with a butterfly back and massive fins which I loved dearly until I replaced it with a vehicle I simply couldn't resist – a '59 Cadillac which I kept for years and which eventually ended up being used in the movie *Superman III*.

Politically, too, there was a change in my life as I personally left the disenfranchised behind me by achieving the ripe old age of twenty-one. Now I could use my voting hand, so meaningfully scarred by Winston's cigar, to take my allotted place in determining who governed my country. My first thought, presumably spurred by my Mentor, was that not only was I entitled to vote – I was also entitled to be voted for. So I decided to form the Sod 'Em All party, which was what I and the people I knew thought of politicians. Most of my music mates, and especially the inhabitants of the Cannibal Pot, thought politics was a load of old bollocks. Some didn't even know who the Prime Minister was, and the rest didn't care. Their attitude was that they were all the same in the end and they were all just trying to nick your money.

There was good reason for this bitterness from people in the music business, and especially from successful pop stars. When they made a hit record, often after years of pounding the circuit for peanuts, they went into the surtax bracket and could lose 95 per cent of their earnings to the state. That was if they hadn't been ripped off in the first place, like Lonnie Donegan who was paid a total of £3 10/- for 'Rock Island Line', a hit which went on selling for years. The taxation blag was bad enough for those artists with a string of hits, but for those with only one in their lifetime it was an absolute disaster, as they would never hit that sort of paydirt again.

In Search of the Lost Chord

By this time I'd made records of my compositions of 'Jack the Ripper', 'All Black and Hairy' and 'My Big Black Coffin' and although they hadn't been big hits I didn't really mind as I hadn't expected them to be. For me the crack was always in doing live gigs, but then making the records had been almost as bizarre as my act. I did the recordings with an extraordinary producer called Joe Meek who had fixed up a studio in his flat over a leather shop in the Holloway Road in north London. Joe was a genius and maverick who had fallen out with the mainstream record companies. They were still incredibly straight and made their engineers wear ties and white coats as if they were doctors, but Joe was much more off the wall and one of the first people to start really experimenting with the art of bending sound.

He got fed up with the big companies and walked out to make his own records, using all kinds of home-made and weird devices to create a unique sound which was a sort of British answer to Phil Spector in America. The set-up in his flat-cum-studio was amazing. There were tape recorders and wires everywhere as always, but what was really peculiar was that Joe would put different sections of the band in different rooms, and even on different floors, whilst he coordinated the whole effect from the living room. Some people would be playing in the bedrooms, others in the kitchen, with maybe one on the stairs. To get the particular echo sound he wanted for one of my records he even made me go into the lavatory and sing with the door shut.

Joe worked with a number of artists, including Johnny Leyton, the Honeycombs, Cliff Bennett and the Rebel Rousers, and Gene Vincent, but the best example of the way he could distort sound in a distinctive way was an instrumental called Telstar, named after the world's first communications satellite, launched in 1962. The recording, played by the Tornados, went to Number One on both sides of the Atlantic.

But Joe had a lot of problems, one of which was being gay at a time when even people with suede shoes were pilloried and he was mortified when his name got into the papers after he was convicted and fined for importuning in a public lavatory. Later in the '60s, as his sound was overtaken by the new groups, he became increasingly depressed and moody. In 1968 he finally snapped and shot his landlady with a 12-bore which Heinz, the Tornados' lead singer, had left at the flat. Then he committed suicide by turning it on himself.

At that moment Joe was flat broke and his only hope had been a successful outcome to the prolonged legal wrangle he had been having with a French composer over the royalties for Telstar, which were massive. Ironically, the court found in Joe's favour a month after he killed himself.

I was amazed as well as shocked and sad when I heard all this, as I had always thought of him as a fabulously successful producer, and it had never occurred to me he had no money and only rented his flat. He was a great man and is still much missed, with an Appreciation Society which continues to meet monthly.

Mac the Knife

As I was happy with my rock'n'horror act, I only vaguely clocked the political scene, which was dominated at the time by that paternalistic old shyster Harold Macmillan, who was keeping himself on top with devious devices like his 'Night of the Long Knives' which decimated the Cabinet. Meanwhile he was turning the Tories into a populist party to cash in on the rise of the plebs and appalling the old guard with his downmarket slogan of 'You've never had it so good'. Us rock and rollers, surrounded by groupies as we were, promptly changed it to 'We've never had it so often!' and continued our fun life on the circuit.

But at the same time something was stirring within me and in 1963 the world changed when President

Kennedy was assassinated in America. I had just got to a gig at Cambridge when I heard the news on the radio and I·announced it at the concert. But it seemed so impossible and was so shocking it was a long time before the audience believed me.

Meanwhile in Britain the Establishment was rocked by the Profumo scandal. Having always understood that the first rule of politics was not to get caught, I realized how low our political currency had fallen now one of our leading politicians had been discovered shagging round the back. Worse, he had then told a pack of lies, or 'terminological inexactitudes' as they are politely known in the political trade, to the House of Commons. Yet at the same time the government had been pompously slagging off teenagers and preaching the importance of responsible behaviour. I had met lots of young people as I toured the country and found myself getting very angry at these double standards.

I remember one particular meeting with a guy and his girl who already had two kids, and she was already pregnant with their third. The Winston spirit was stirring within me and we were talking about politics when I impulsively announced I was thinking of standing for Parliament. They replied they wished they could vote for me, but they couldn't because they were only twenty. I thought how ridiculous that was: these parents of a family, the most important thing in the world because it was for the rest of your life – as well as ensuring the next generation of voters – were considered old enough to have children and to be called up and die for their country – not to mention buy my records – but not old enough to vote.

It's My Party

There and then I resolved to form a political party, which I said I wanted all teenagers to join. Scrubbing the Sod 'Em All party, my childhood memory was rekindled and I decided to call it the Winston Churchill party. But all my friends pointed out that voters would think I was some sort of independent Tory, so I settled on the more straightforward title of the National Teenage party.

There were several strands to my thinking. Rock and roll was arousing enormous controversy with the teddy boys swaggering down the streets. The way youth seemed to be taking over was causing consternation and some of this concern was justified as things could get pretty rough. I had continued with boxing after school by going to the Rotex club in Willesden and always had to keep my wits about me as you were never sure, being from outside the area, when the Willesden mob might attack you. I was also privileged to witness the Great South Ruislip Punch-Up when an army of teds, all tooled up with clubs and bicycle chains, marched on the nearby US base because the Yanks had been pinching their girlfriends. The massed ranks of teds in their black drainpipes and drape jackets were an awesome and frightening sight, but they blew it when they foolishly allowed themselves to be lured inside the base. Once inside, and on American territory, they had the shit beaten out of them by the Military Police.

The first reaction of the older generation to all these goings-on had been to bury their heads in the sand by saying rock and roll would only be a two-minute wonder. When that proved wrong they changed their line to labelling it as the devil's music. My mates and I found ourselves denounced as lunatics and madmen and terrified parents were wound up by claims in the press that we were coming to get their daughters. In many cases this last accusation was true, but I can assure you the daughters were only too glad to see us, especially in the dozens of one-horse towns where there was never anything else to do.

The Establishment and the papers then changed their attack to making out that we were all so thick we couldn't string two words together. This snobbery was founded on the fact that most successful pop stars were working class and had only a minimal education, like myself. But it was a gross insult, as well as being quite untrue. Rock and roll was three words for a start, and we could all wrap our tongues round 'be-bop-a-lu-la' a damn sight better than they could. In many cases the people who were grumbling were as thick as pigshit themselves, and even worse educated than us. I could see how galling it must have been for them to watch us take control of our lives and have so much fun. But I wanted to prove to them that rock and roll – and teenagers – were here to stay. New music and fashions were bursting on the scene almost daily and trendy people were already starting to talk excitedly about the 'Swinging '60s'. As the first young generation with money to spend, we were rapidly becoming the kings of the consumer society.

The Young Ones

I decided there would be nowhere better for me to make my stand than in the by-election at Stratford-upon-Avon caused by Profumo's resignation from Parliament. I wasn't sure about Stratford as a town, as I'd always found it very poor for rock and roll, but I did agree with the Bard that music was the food of love and I was most definitely in favour of playing on. But when I went down to register as a candidate I found the procedure and paperwork quite baffling, so I called up Reg Calvert, my old promoter in the Two I's days, who lived not far away in Rugby. Reg assured me he knew all about 'the red tape and the bullshit' through his dealings with local councils. 'They make it as complicated as arseholes so you get all confused and don't bother,' he told me. 'Leave it all to me. I'll sort through the mess for you.' Reg proved as good as his word and I soon got myself nominated.

Until that point it had never really occurred to me I was the first rock and roll singer to stand for Parliament. In those days the very idea of an outside candidate was quite unusual and when it was a wild, Loony person known as the most outlandish of all the pop stars, it was considered completely off the wall. Just the bald fact of being on the ballot paper put me on the front page.

The Establishment had already been rocked enough by the Profumo scandal and the revelations of Christine Keeler and Mandy Rice-Davies. *Private Eye* and satirical shows like 'That Was the Week That Was' were causing further embarrassment and the last thing the system needed was somebody like me getting into the actual electoral mix. I soon became a *cause célèbre*

42

and the subject of letters to *The Times* and other big papers from indignant colonel-types and several Messrs 'Disgusted of Tunbridge Wells'.

To become a candidate I had to pay a deposit of £150, which was a lot of money then. But I was on a good screw with my gigs and for me it was only the equivalent of a week's work. Being very new to the game I also made the first mistake of actually believing I had a good chance of saving my deposit. My excitement knew no bounds when I was a lead item on Pathe News, the old black and white newsreel led off by a cock crowing. Pathe went round all the cinemas and was very influential at a time when plenty of households still did not have a television. I was convinced it would swing me a lot of votes.

Whole Lotta Shakin' Goin' On

To copy the example of the big parties I hired a hall and put an ad in the local paper announcing an election meeting. I'd never even been to one before, but Reg assured me they were low-key events and we'd only get the press and a few punters. So I wasn't feeling nervous as I set up a table on the stage and wrapped a few posters round the front like you're supposed to. I placed a jug of water on the table and a couple of glasses on top and made sure the beer bottles were well out of sight as we opened for business.

To my amazement we pulled a full house of four hundred or so people. If it had been a gig the joint would have been rocking, but as it was I was petrified. I had never given a speech in my life and at my gigs I was used to having a band behind me. Standing there with no music or accompaniment was very different, and I knew straight away it was going to be a rough ride.

The audience was so hostile I suspected the other parties had sent in professional hecklers. Most of the faces in front of me looked like typical posh, smug Tories and some people were hanging on my every word before jumping straight up to pick holes in my policies. As soon as I opened my mouth they started shouting remarks like: 'What a load of old rubbish!' 'How could these half-witted rock and roll kids run the country?' 'What a load of tosh!' One fat squire-type with a handlebar moustache got so carried away he leapt on to his chair and bounced up and down scratching his armpits and chanting: 'The apes are taking over! The apes are taking over!' He got a cheap laugh at the time, but I got the last one when a photograph of him looking ridiculous was printed in the local rag.

With fools like him having a go the meeting soon degenerated into a shambles and as the uproar mounted I knew I wasn't handling it very well. I was frustrated by being stuck in one place on the stage rather than being able to leap about, and my legs started turning to lead. How I longed for a Fender Stratocaster CS and a 500-watt Marshall amp to blast them into submission – never mind giving them a mega-version of my pig's head and guts routine!

These Boots Are Made For Walking

The only way out seemed to be to get back on the streets where I felt more at home. So, off the top of my head, I announced a march for the next day, starting at

Shakespeare's old gaff, and closed the meeting. There were huge groans at this abrupt end to the fun, but at least I'd got myself temporarily out of the spotlight.

The next day my followers and I met up at Anne Hathaway's cottage as arranged. They were a colourful crew – lots of girls wearing miniskirts and people with all sorts of silly hats and clothes and banners and placards proclaiming my slogans of 'Parliament will be screaming if you vote Lord Sutch!', 'Vote Sutch and gain much!' and 'Vote for the Ghoul. He's no Fool!'

It was like no political parade Stratford had ever seen, with someone banging a drum and another blowing his own trumpet, on the grounds that was what politicians did. The march had sparked off huge media interest and as more and more cameras turned up I set off with no real plan except to head towards the local high street. But the whole show was so exciting and colourful, people started joining in and soon the march was so large it was being flanked by policemen hurriedly called in to stop the traffic. We might have walked to Birmingham except nobody, including me, had the faintest idea where we were going. As I was leading, this was a problem. But I had to smile as I reflected how in character it was for a true politician to march his supporters down the road to nowhere.

Eventually, of course, I got lost down the sidestreets and matters came to a head when I turned a corner into a cul-de-sac and came smack up against the canal bank. Faced with no choice, I stopped and everybody ended up in a tangled heap as the rank and file piled in from behind. It was total chaos, but we all thought it great fun.

It was after this that the campaign got rougher still and I found myself under deep suspicion from the local burghers, many of whom I suspected were not above a little shagging round the back themselves. Angus Maude, the Tory candidate, treated me like vermin from another planet and studiously avoided me. This did not surprise me so much, but I was puzzled that even Tory canvassers in the street scuttled away if I so much as looked at them. Then it dawned on me that they were frightened of being photographed with me in case it made them look ridiculous. I fought back by protesting I was merely giving voice to opinion, and it was a free world. When they still turned their backs on me I accused them of refusing to enter the debate, thereby proving I was the only one with the guts to do the job, but they still ran away.

Running Bear

However, the most bitter attack of all did not come from the Tories, but a huge guy with a beard who looked like a cross between Rasputin and Henry VIII. This extraordinary sight, it was reverentially pointed out to me, was Andrew Faulds, the Shakespearean actor, who was standing as the Labour candidate. Faulds wasn't too bad to start with and we seemed to get on all right. But things changed when a newspaper cartoon appeared saying you had to be an actor or a singer to be in this by-election. He turned out to be as paranoid about being bracketed with me as the Tories and immediately denounced me for trying to turn a serious business into a joke.

Stung by this attack, and curious to see what sort of an edge being an actor gave him, I went to one of his outdoor meetings to study his effect on the crowd. I found him bellowing at them as if he was in a Shakespearean play, but as he was addressing a typical cross-section of the population, with mums with pushchairs and scruffy little kids running about, his grand words were going completely over their heads.

'Friends, Stratfordians and countrymen, lend me your ears,' this wild dishevelled figure was shouting. 'To vote, or not to vote, that is the question. Whether 'tis nobler to suffer the slings and arrows of outrageous fortune, or to take arms against a sea of Tories, and by opposing, end them . . . Once more unto the breach, dear friends . . .'

After the newspaper cartoon Faulds had been so rude about me I felt entitled to have a word, so I interrupted with a cheerful cry of: 'Cool it, man! It's only an election, after all!'

He swung round like a huge bull, bellowing with rage and so uptight I thought I should lay a quote on him from the great Bard of Rock – Elvis Presley. I often turn to the King's golden words myself when things go wrong and my choice for Faulds was the recitation from the song Elvis always said was his personal favourite, 'Are You Lonesome Tonight?'

'As a singer, Shakespeare's not really my bag,' I told him. 'But I think you should hear this, as I believe it may help you, as it has often helped me.'

Striking my Elvis impersonation pose I then lowered my voice to a rough approximation of my idol's deep croon. 'Andrew, I wonder if you're lonesome tonight?' I intoned, buckling at the knees as I spread my arms out towards him. 'You know, Andrew,' I continued, 'someone once said "The world's a stage, and each must play a part . . ."'

For some reason, the second he heard the King's

immortal words Faulds turned purple with rage. 'Out, out, damned spot!' he shrieked. 'Out, vile jelly! Stand not upon the order of your going, but go at once!'

Little Things (That You Do)

Deciding Faulds was a hopeless case, and anyway that there was little point in canvassing for Shakespeare's vote as he'd been dead for four hundred years, I switched camps and went to one of Maude's meetings, which was much more what I'd been led to expect. It was as dull as a vicar's tea party and the high point came when Maude paused during his speech to take a sip of water.

I noticed with satisfaction that the handful of people nodding off seemed to find it as boring as I did, but it was obviously what they expected from their candidate as Maude won comfortably, with Faulds trailing well behind. I'd hardly expected anything else, as the seat was a Tory stronghold, but I was pleased to find Profumo's old majority had been severely cut. It was obvious that many of the Tory voters had agreed with me about the shagging round the back and the lying business and not voted as a protest.

For myself I got 208 votes – a shattering disappointment after my ludicrously high expectations. But then I cheered up. It was, I thought, a considerable achievement to have found 208 people mad enough to vote for me in somewhere as straight as Stratford. For my platform had one serious Loony flaw in electoral terms – the very people I was representing, eighteen to twenty-one year olds, were unable to put their cross on the ballot paper.

But all in all my political blooding had been quite a shock. For the moment, after the way I'd been treated by the other candidates, I was only interested in getting back to the comparatively sane world of rock and roll.

SMOKE GETS IN YOUR EYES

AS THE '60s really began to swing I found myself happily placed. Everybody had thought I was mad and I'd been labelled a two-minute wonder and pasted by some of the music critics. But I had made some money, which I put down as a deposit on a big house called . White Lodge in Watford Road, Harrow, which had four bedrooms and a double garage. I'd also bought a bungalow nearby for Mum and now, to my great satisfaction, someone else cleaned our windows.

The whole point as I'd always seen it was the act I'd put together was essentially visual, and as such was evergreen. I had noticed that many of the people in the business considered to be really wild and woolly were in fact quite flat-footed and seriously alarmed at my antics. But that hadn't stopped me building up a regular circuit round Britain playing places like Granadas and co-op and town halls, where I regularly topped the bill to houses of anything from five hundred to two thousand people.

There were other interesting diversions to famous venues like the Star Club in Hamburg, where I ran into the Beatles in their early days and had some long chats with John Lennon, who was tickled by the theatrical side of my act and predicted a long life for it.

Rave On

The Raving Savages, however, were not so steady. Band members came and went with alarming regularity and through the years a number progressed on to great fame. The band was a brilliant showcase for any talented young musician trying to break into the big time. With its high profile it always attracted interest and there was a continuous stream of press articles about how outrageous it all was. There were also all sorts of spin-offs, like my being given the Golden Hairnet Award along with Mick Jagger and Prince Charles, which was some sort of bollocks promoted by safety at work people.

Whenever one of the Savages was offered a big break I had to let him go, if only because I couldn't match the money on offer. But there was always a queue of good musicians waiting to step into the line-up which, at its peak, had two female backing singers (dressed as vampires, naturally) and four saxophones. With that I could blow off any competition.

Mick Jagger and Brian Jones became big fans and poached Carlo Little, Nicky Hopkins and Rick Brown for the first Rolling Stones line-up. When Carlo decided to pack it in he leant over to Jagger, picked up a fag packet and wrote 'Charlie Watts' and a phone number on it. The rest is history.

Nick Simper and Ritchie Blackmore left me to join Deep Purple; Noel Redding went to play bass for Jimi Hendrix with Mitch Mitchell as his drummer; Jeff Beck was with me for a time; and then there was Matthew Fisher, our organist after Nicky Hopkins. Matt used to warm up by playing classical music, with Carlo shouting at him that we were a rock and roll band and he'd piss all the punters off by trying to educate them. The next thing we knew he'd gone as organist to another group and they soon released the classic smash hit, 'A Whiter Shade of Pale', as Procul Harum.

The most handsome of all, and the guy who got all the girls, was another piano player, Paul Nicholas, star of the successful TV comedies 'Just Good Friends' and 'Close to Home'. Paul was incredibly good looking and we always used him to lure the girls right up to the front of the stage, though he himself was terrified by a lot of what we did. But he was not so much a musician as a singer and actor, and from the Savages he went on to take the leads in *Hair* and *Jesus Christ Superstar* before moving to *Grease* and then *Cats* and starring in a number of films. Paul was later quoted as saying: 'Appearing naked in *Hair* was nothing compared to playing keyboards for Screaming Lord Sutch wearing only a leotard!'

All Along the Watchtower

Whilst the Raving Savages and I were pounding the circuit pressing the outrage button, a different agenda was being set on radio, where the nation was groaning under the tyrannical regime of the one-party state of the BBC and its hated commissars like David Jacobs and Jimmy Young. In those days of the Light Programme and the Home Service the choice for the people was appalling. The big numbers were programmes like 'Workers' Playtime' and 'Music While You Work', designed for a population still chained to factory benches and housework.

The bland strains of Victor Sylvester echoed everywhere alongside the mindless honky-tonk of the nine-fingered pianist Russ Conway, and the height of excitement was the Billy Cotton Bandshow with its idiotic catchline of 'Wakey Wakey!'

Television was no better. The nation was stupefied in front of programmes like the 'Black and White Minstrel Show' and was pole-axed by crooners such as Ronnie Hilton, Alma Cogan, and Pearl Carr and Teddy Johnson, and with Frankie Vaughan waving his topper about as the only visible sign of life.

Radio Luxemburg, which had first beamed rock and roll into Britain from Europe, was still young people's only hope as they battled with its fading reception to hear the kind of music they wanted until the scene was abruptly transformed by the arrival of the pirate radio stations, which escaped the regulations by broadcasting from ships moored offshore, outside territorial waters. It was the pirates, particularly Radio Caroline and Radio London, who were the real pioneers in breaking the Swinging '60s scene. The BBC continued to be very sniffy about rock and roll or anything new in the field of pop. I had particular cause for resentment as the Corp had always banned my records, like anything they found unusual or threatening.

After my Stratford experience I decided, unlike other politicians, to practise what I preached. As I believed in commercial radio and thought it should be legalized as it was in America and Australia, I started up Radio Sutch as a protest. The transmitter for this mighty denizen of the airwaves was originally installed on a fishing smack called the *Cornucopia*, which was then anchored off Shoeburyness in the Thames estuary. Unfortunately the boat was only insured for fishing

The ludicrous list of records the Beeb advised local radio stations not to play during the Gulf War.

Elton John's 'Saturday Night's Alright For Fighting'
Status Quo's 'In the Army Now'
Lulu's 1969 hit 'Boom Bang a Bang'
Phil Collins's love song 'In the Air Tonight'
Abba's 1974 hit 'Waterloo'
'Killer Queen' by Queen
'I Shot the Sheriff' by Eric Clapton
'Atomic' by Blondie
'The Israelites' by Desmond Dekker
'Walk Like an Egyptian' and 'Billy, Don't Be
    a Hero' by the Bangles
'Two Tribes' by Frankie Goes to Hollywood
'(I Just) Died in Your Arms' by Cutting Crew
'Light My Fire' by the Doors
'Under Attack' by Abba
'Imagine' by John Lennon
'Fields of Fire' by Big Country
'Silent Running' by Mike and the Mechanics
'Love Is a Battlefield' by Pat Benatar
'War' by Edwin Starr

Most ridiculous of all was 'Give Peace a Chance' by John Lennon.

Yet at the same time the British Forces Broadcasting Service reported the most requested records by the men on the spot were Cher's 'Bang Bang', Jona Lewie's 'Stop the Cavalry', and Barry Maguire's classic 'Eve of Destruction'.

Plus ça change!

and not music, so I had to abandon this horn of plenty for an old wartime seafort which stood on rusty iron legs eight miles off the coast near Herne Bay at a place called Shivering Sands. The name was very apt.

Technically Radio Sutch was somewhat crude and heavy-duty lorry batteries featured largely in the action. But as usual I took matters one step further than anyone else by broadcasting excerpts from the 'naughty books' *Fanny Hill* and *Lady Chatterley's Lover*. The jury in the Lady Chatterley obscenity trial had recently been asked whether it was the sort of book they would want their servants to read and I thought the servants should have a chance to decide that for themselves. The press remarked how fishing boats would circle the fort at serial times, which gives you some idea of the range of our transmitter.

Such a bold stroke was bound to cause controversy and, alarmed by the enormous depth of my political appeal, the authorities despatched a task force to shut me down. I resisted valiantly for a few days as I was already in the last stages of planning Sutch Island, which was to be a nudist colony with its own stamps and currency. But despite my pirate rig and the cutlass from my act which I brandished at boarders, I was finally forced to surrender in order to avoid bloodshed. Although I was evacuated at least I was satisfied that I had made my point.

Little Red Rooster

Meanwhile the political scene changed dramatically when Macmillan was replaced by the ghastly Sir Alec

Douglas-Home, with his aristocratic manner and skull-like appearance. Spotting Home was so absolutely tailor-made for my horror band he wouldn't even need make-up, I invited him for an audition, but he never showed – I think it was probably because the money wasn't good enough. Douglas-Home lived in a world where ordinary people were relegated to being serfs and beaters on grouse moors and he soon lost the 1964 General Election to Harold Wilson. Still basking in my Stratford and Radio Sutch success, I stayed out of this, naively expecting things would get better after Labour had won.

Then, in January 1965, my Mentor, Winston Churchill, died. I watched his funeral on tenterhooks, fearful my Inheritance would be revealed in his will and the eyes of the world would turn upon me. But in his wisdom Winnie had kept our secret, and it didn't take me long to suss out that, for all his smarmy talk, Wilson was just like any other politician and would need a kick up the arse before he would do anything.

By now the hippies had arrived, and at my concerts I found myself being enveloped by the heady atmosphere from the grass roots. As my senses reeled under the joint attack of my people's favoured substances, Winnie's voice rang through my head, urging me once more to stand up and be counted. So when Harold called another General Election in 1966 I put myself up against him in his home constituency of Huyton in Lancashire. Again I stood for National Teenage party, but this time, as well as campaigning for votes at eighteen, I expanded my platform to include the legalization of commercial radio.

At Stratford I'd found many people amazed I could be a candidate as they believed only toffs could stand in elections – part of the doffing of the cap attitude encouraged to keep the workers in their correct place. So I led off my campaign – using a little political licence so as not to give away the Winnie inheritance with him just gone – by stating I was a candidate 'to prove that anyone – dustman, roadsweeper, whoever – could stand for Parliament'.

Dedicated Follower of Fashion

After my run-in at Stratford with the political pygmies of Maude and Faulds, I knew Wilson would be sterner opposition. And, as he was obviously skilled in the art of stretching thin material, I thought I ought to get a few tips from the old master himself.

At Stratford I'd worn the morning coat and topper to keep things straight and Winston-fashion and to fit in with the toff thinking. Now I contemplated changing to the Lurex leopardskin from my rock and roll act. Sartorially I had decided this would look suitably outrageous, and it would also show a sincerity which would appeal to deeper-thinking punters. A leopard cannot change its spots, so symbolically I would be indicating how I was not going to chop and change with the winds of fortune. And I would also be showing that, unlike other politicians, I didn't claim to be spotless. Even with Winnie's mantle I didn't consider myself 100 per cent perfect. Only, I calculated, I was about 99.99 per cent of the way there. Finally, wearing leopardskin would signal what I believed – that politicians were an endangered species destined to have less and less control over people's lives. As Bob Dylan had been telling America: 'The times they are a'changing . . .'

With all that deep significance, I concluded, I might at least get a few *Guardian* readers to vote for me.

Raindrops Keep Falling on My Head

With the unthinking bravado of youth I just picked up the phone and rang Wilson at Downing Street to invite myself round. Always a supreme opportunist with an eye to the main chance, he cautiously agreed to see me, although he insisted it was to be at an inconspicuous grotty pub nearby. I met him as arranged and sat him down in the snug to explain my dilemma.

'Tha' must be bloody daft, lad,' Harold replied in his bluff northern way, noisily supping on a pint of trade-union-approved Federation bitter and slapping dollops of brown HP sauce on his pie. 'Tha'll end up neither muckling nor mickling if tha' messes about like that!' he continued through a mouthful. 'Tek it from me, lad, tha' should stick to t'cloth-cap image for t' punters like I do. Tha'll ne'er get anywhere wi' leopardskin – it's too way out.' Stuffing in more pie he added: 'Anyhow, you daft young get, everybody knows t'leopards can't vote!'

Reaching down to the seat beside him he held up a grubby raincoat with a curious sort of collar. 'Take a look at this, lad,' he said. 'This 'ere is a Gannex, assembled by craftsmen in t'northern metropolis of Leeds and t'greatest raincoat in t'world. Feel t'width, lad,' he urged me, pressing the garment into my hands. 'It's a good buy, tha' knows. Try them nice deep pockets – just right for t'pipe and t'tobacco tin!

'I may be t'top politician in Britain,' he concluded with a self-satisfied smile, 'but even I'll admit I can't

stop it raining in this bloody country. But there's one
thing I can do though, which is mek sure everybody
'as a mac like this to keep theirsens dry. Yon's caring
socialism for thee!'

Naively taking his advice, that afternoon I attended
Burton's Gentlemen's Outfitters and bought one. I was
a bit puzzled by a label reading 'SHOWERPROOF ONLY DO
NOT USE IN HEAVY STORMS', but as the sun was shining
I thought it safe to give it an airing.

Do-Wa-Diddy-Diddy-Dum-Diddy-Do

Sweating slightly, I made for one of my familiar haunts
in Carnaby Street, where I bumped into my old mate
Adam Faith. But even though I'd just finished a tour
with him, at first he didn't seem to recognize me as I
shuffled towards him.

Then he creased up. 'God Almighty!' he shouted,
reeling back and clutching a passing hippy for support.
'David, is that really you? You look just like that old
fart Harold Wilson!' Still cackling with laughter he
pulled me into Lord John's boutique. 'Look what the
cat brought in!' he shouted as a young female assistant
came up to serve me.

'Wow! How totally unhip can you get, man?' she
replied excitedly. 'Hey, you must be one of those
plebs from the northern kitchen sink dramas! I really
dig the look!'

Realizing I had been conned by Harold I stood there
red-faced and cursing as the trendy customers gathered
round and mocked the vile garment. To retrieve the
situation I quickly selected a few off the peg items –
a purple corduroy suit with a fashionable box jacket,

embossed pink and black shirt sporting the latest line in long pointed collars, and a flower-power tie with a pattern of green and yellow swirls.

Feeling my old self again, I emerged back into the youthful throng carrying the odious Gannex in a plastic bag, and was accosted by an old tramp. 'Give a poor old man something to him keep him warm, guv,' he pleaded.

'I've got just the thing for you, squire,' I replied, producing the raincoat and thrusting it at him. But he seemed suspicious as he expertly felt the hem with his gnarled fingers.

'It's got nice big pockets to keep your dog-ends in,' I pointed out, unconsciously echoing Harold's sales patter. But the old man did not seem convinced and ignored me as he picked at the stitching and examined the collar with a look of distaste. Eventually he gave a dismissive sniff, rolled the coat into a ball and with unerring accuracy chucked it into the nearest litter bin.

I Shot the Sheriff

My campaign against Harold in Huyton went well. The constituency was close to Liverpool where the music scene was roaring and there was a lot of support for my radio policy. I attended the count in a state of high excitement to find much more atmosphere than at dull old Stratford. The jubilation when Harold was dutifully elected by his faithful voters was immense, for by then the Swingometer on the telly had moved pendulum-like in Labour's favour and everybody knew he would be the next PM.

As Harold stood amongst the debris of the count grinning like a Cheshire Cat, the only thing marring his enjoyment was that he could not get his new pocket calculator working. He was cursing about 'that damn fool Benn and his bloody white heat of technology' when Mary, who had broken off from composing one of her poems for a moment, leaned over and pressed the 'On' button for him.

She gave me the poem afterwards, and I still treasure it today:

> Harold has won the election,
> And we return to Number 10,
> But David is Sutch a nice, nice boy
> I hope we meet him again!

Harold wasn't the only one with something to celebrate. I had got a staggering 585 votes, 277 more than at Stratford, and was therefore well chuffed. So when the Conservative agent unexpectedly produced a box of cigars and offered them round I happily took one. As I did so I observed it had already been lit and half-smoked before being stubbed out. For a moment I thought this was typical Tory meanness and then the penny dropped. This was no ordinary cigar – it was a talisman being passed to me by the Conservatives, an acknowledgement that now dear old Winnie had gone I was to step into his shoes.

Puff the Magic Dragon

The cigar I was now holding was obviously one the Great Man had smoked himself. I just knew it had

61

been touched by his lips. Possibly, I thought with a sudden thrill, it was the very one he had stubbed out on my infant hand so many years ago! I took it and held it for a second, rubbing the rough leaf against the scar my Mentor had left on my palm, and which I still have today. Then I had a mischievous thought, which I knew would have made Winnie laugh.

Harold was shuffling away, trying to avoid the photo-opportunity he could see coming, so I reached out and patted him on the shoulder. As he swung round I uttered my immortal line, hamming up a broad Cockney accent to rub it in: ''Ow's about a light then, eh, 'Arold?'

Wilson was stymied. As aware of the significance of the moment as I, he fumbled in his jacket pocket and got out his lighter. With a knowing look in his beady eye he clicked it into life.

'Ee, tha's a crafty young bugger!' I heard the old charlatan mutter as he saw me upstaging his main prop. I smiled condescendingly, savouring the moment even more because I knew his secret – he personally enjoyed smoking cigars in private, but never did so in public so as not to upset his 'ordinary man' image.

'Thank you and good luck, because you're going to need it in the tricky waters that lie ahead,' I replied. 'There are spies everywhere, you know.'

'Tha's right there, lad!' he muttered back furtively. 'There's a plot in MI5, tha' knows, to mek me out to be a bloody Communist.' He looked at me shiftily and added: 'And that's a bit bloody rich when I'm not even a bloody socialist! I reckon it's all down to t'Third Man. Y'see, I wa' talkin' to M t'other day – y'know, 'e's the bloke in charge – and he told me he'd put 'is top agent – that James Bond bloke – on t'case but I reckon . . .'

Bored by his familiar paranoia I turned away, pulling on the Havana until the end glowed cherry red. As I did so I knew this wasn't mere tobacco smoke I was inhaling – it was the very essence of Winnie. As if a genie was emerging from a bottle, I felt myself possessed. Winnie came within me, his spirit permeating deep into my lungs and the very marrow of my bones.

The next day a picture of the historic cigar moment appeared on the front page of the *New York Times*, relaying the same signal to our old wartime allies. My record label, Atlantic, promptly cabled me to say that they couldn't work out how I'd done it – even the great Ray Charles couldn't hit those heights, they said!

Please Please Me

Harold must have found me useful, for a few weeks later he rang me up and invited me round to the pub again, where I found he had dimly picked up on the importance of pop music to young people.

'Y'know Mary and I are great fans of these new-fangled groups – t'Earwigs, t'Rolling Moss, Gerry and t'Transplants, Cilla Purple, never mind that Elvis Richard and Cliff Presley,' he explained. 'What I need to know, lad, is where it's all 'appening, like – somewhere where I can be top of t'political pops.'

I hastily recommended the Cavern in Liverpool so as to keep him away from my mates at the Two I's, where his appearance as one of my hangers-on would be catastrophic.

'T'Cavern,' Wilson mused, puffing on his smelly pipe. 'A right dark 'ole, is it? Well, that sorta place

suits me fine. Ee! And it's just down t'road from me
punters so it proves it must be just oop me street. I'll
tell Lady Falkender to book me in.'

We Are the Champions

'Is there owt else I can do for t'youth?' he asked,
supping more Federation. I briefly considered a Beatles
haircut but after giving him a quick once-over rejected
the idea.

'Why not dish out a few Honours to a pop group?'
I suggested instead. 'It won't cost you any brass and
it'll show how fab you are.'

'Good idea, lad,' he replied, slapping his knee. 'I'm
fed oop wi' giving 'em to knackered old trade unionists
and them useless buggers in t'kitchen cabinet. Now,
let me do thee a favour in return by giving thee a
good tip,' he went on. I waited for details of his latest
slagheap scam, but this time it wasn't another dodgy
land deal. Instead Harold put his lips next to my ear,
singeing the collar of my Regency jacket with the bowl
of his pipe, and whispered dramatically: 'I've fixed
it so England will beat t'Germans at football to win
t'World Coop! A week is a long time in politics, lad,
and I've got to show t'punters Winston might have
beaten Germans in t'war, but it takes an 'Arold to beat
'em in peacetime!'

Leaning back and blowing clouds of blue smoke from
his pipe he continued: 'Y'see, it's me master plan to
keep t'plebs 'appy. I told 'em I'd look after t'pound in
their pocket but then I fooked that oop by devaluing
t'ruddy thing. So now I'm arranging t'soccer success
instead to show how Labour looks after t'interests

of t'working man.' Grinning, he downed the last of his pint of bitter and let out a small belch before adding: 'Mark my words, lad – stick a bet on and tha'll clean oop!'

After the Gannex episode, I foolishly didn't believe him. But when England improbably beat Germany I realized just how devious the world of politics was. Harold, I saw, was a political Arthur Daley, using anything and anybody – from me to our national game – in the constant wheeling and dealing which kept him on top. If that was politics, I thought, give me good old rock and roll anytime. Altogether I was pissed off with England and its narrow little world.

Finally, in May 1973 the government bowed to pressure and legalized commercial radio but at the time it simply shut the pirates down in an operation led by Anthony Wedgwood Benn, then Postmaster General. As Benn was always banging on about censorship that was ironical enough, but worse still was how cynical the stitch-up was. The pirates' best DJs like Tony Blackburn, Kenny Everett, Dave Lee Travis and Johnny Walker were promptly nicked by the BBC, which was then revamped whilst staying as Establishment-minded as ever.

Seeing all this, like so many before me from the Pilgrim Fathers onwards, I determined to say a temporary goodbye to these shores and seek my fortune in the USA. Over there no British politicians would step on my blue suede shoes and I could also fulfil my greatest ambition by meeting the King – Elvis Aaron Presley.

CALIFORNIA DREAMIN'

AS WELL as wanting a break from England, I had other things on my mind. After such a successful start in politics, I found myself examining my motives. What was my driving force? What was it, as they say, that made me run? One answer was baked beans, but that was not the answer I was looking for. I pondered the equation as I knocked round my regular haunts of Carnaby Street and the Portobello Road, envying the simple life of sex, drugs, and rock and roll which I had enjoyed until my political awakening.

Wrestling with my subconscious, I sought the truth behind my actions. I'd always had a low opinion of politicians as a species, now I feared that underneath I might be as frail as all the others, in the game for some tawdry bauble like a minor honour, or if I licked enough boots, a knighthood or peerage. I'd always been more of a Rolling Stones than a Beatles fan, but I had to admire the Liverpool lads for showing us musicians were made of sterner stuff by sending back the OBEs Wilson had awarded them on my advice. Harold really was the pits amongst my mates, and I was struck by the awful thought he might now award me some similar sort of recognition, thereby destroying my musical career.

To prevent this happening I made the pre-emptive strike of taking my stage-name and making it official by changing my name to Lord by deed-poll. Whilst I was at it I also took the title of the Fifth Earl of Harrow, designing myself a tasteful coat of arms with a motto of: 'They shall get stuffed'. Now I could be on equal terms with anyone and everyone in a society where, despite everything the Harolds of this world had promised, some were plainly more equal than others.

Give Peace a Chance

Still trying to find my sense of direction, I studied Winston's career for further clues. As he had only reached the top by starting the Second World War I asked my fellow rockers if I should also go to such lengths. The answer was a universal thumbs-down. I had nicknamed the musicians who left the Savages my 'Ambassadors of Rock' as I watched them spreading my message round the world. But by now the backdrop to which we all played had changed completely. Pop music is very much a generation thing, and for me and my contemporaries there would never be anyone to beat the great names of the late '50s we grew up with. Chuck Berry has to be my Number One, not just because of his distinctive sound, but because he wrote such great lyrics. Then of course there is Elvis. But the hippies had stolen one of the main planks of my act. I was no longer an isolated long-hair and the changes in music were now being summed up by the psychedelia of the Beatles' album, *Sergeant Pepper's Lonely Hearts Club Band*.

The year of 1967 had been dubbed the 'Summer of Love' and Mick Jagger had invited me to the Rolling Stones' free concert in Hyde Park, where a mass of butterflies were released in memory of Brian Jones, who had just died. Brian and I had been old muckers and I had always particularly admired his habit of sitting on the floor when we went to posh Chelsea parties. But I had always felt there was something strange about him – as if he was searching for something he would never find.

The message now was 'peace, man' and John Lennon advised me: 'Make love, not war.' But sadly I knew bringing peace was as much beyond me as any other politician. And I was also torn by another worry: was I in danger of peaking too early? Harold had taken note of my campaign and was lowering the age for voters to eighteen, and I feared that if things continued like this I would be in grave danger of being taken seriously. All in all, it was time to head west.

Broken English

As a kid I had always bought boxing magazines like the *Ring* and *Sports Illustrated* and been addicted to American comics, especially the classic DC series like *Superman*. Then when Elvis Presley came along, I knew one day I had to go to America. In my dreams I would step off the boat and all my heroes would be there waiting for me. They weren't, of course, but I still arrived in New York at the beginning of 1968 to an enthusiastic press reception. I'd decided to travel in style by sailing across the Atlantic on the *Queen Elizabeth*, taking my own car, a 1955 long-wheelbase Rolls-Royce Silver Wraith with Park Ward bodywork. I'd bought it from an undertakers up north as a sure way of getting a car that hadn't been thrashed to death.

The Rolls was my pride and joy and hugely empha-
sized my new Official Lordliness, while to display
my patriotic fervour I had had the Union Jack painted
on it. The interior was equipped with leopardskin
seat covers. I was photographed with the Rolls on the
dockside in all my Regency finery and hailed as one
of the 'second wave' of British musicians taking
America by storm after the Stones and the Beatles, as
I arrived on the same day as the Animals and Jimi
Hendrix.

Hendrix, in my view, was not only one of the
greatest musicians ever, but one of the hardest done
by. He had been discovered in America, brought across
to England and was now returning to the States in
triumph along with two of my ex-Savages, Noel Redding
on bass and 'Mitch' Mitchell on drums, as the Jimi
Hendrix Experience. I saw all three of them from time
to time throughout that tour and although they were
staying in the best hotels and could order anything
they liked, they never actually had any money of their
own. The reason for this only became apparent later
when it was discovered that practically everything had
been ripped off before Jimi died.

In theory both Noel and Mitch were owed millions,
but they never saw a penny and it was not until the
end of the '80s that Mitch got something out of it.
Jimi had left the guitar he had used at the Isle of
Wight festival at Mitch's house and he finally decided
to auction it. It went in with a reserve of £20,000, but
by the time it had been bid up to £180,000 Mitch was
so overwhelmed he had left the room. 'It was Jimi's
way of paying me back,' he told me afterwards.

My rock'n'horror show went down well in the States,
and I played a series of good clubs round New York and

New England, with the audiences boosted by my live performances on the Merv Griffin, Johnny Carson and Dick Clarke TV shows.

Get Your Kicks on Route 66

Like many British people who go to America I liked many aspects of the country. It was refreshing to find people who were not frightened of being rich, and the way it was acceptable to flaunt your wealth struck me particularly because of their attitude toward my Roller. In Britain you got sneered at and people scratched the paintwork out of spite, but Americans didn't see anything wrong. It just reinforced their determination to have one themselves.

The Roller was the key to the other side of my American adventure, as I was not only playing music but also batting for the country as part of the 'I'm Backing Britain' campaign promoted by the 'Bouncing Czech', Robert Maxwell. My job was to publicize British fashions made by my Carnaby Street mates and I had samples from shops like Lord Kitchener's Valet, Lord John and Carnaby Cavern as well as some I'd designed myself. It was all the Regency dandy look, with red riding jackets in velvet brocade, Napoleon-style jackets with braiding on the coats and pockets made from genuine gold and taken from admirals' suits, flared trousers, cuban-heeled leather shoes, cravats and even silk top hats. To round off the effect I carried a period swordstick, which I found a handy defence against folk music fanatics. I put all this stuff in a little trailer I'd bought through *Exchange and Mart* from a farmer who'd used it to carry pigs and which hooked neatly on to the back of the Roller.

Thus equipped I travelled the breadth of the country, something I'd always wanted to do, going first to the area around Chicago and Milwaukee, through Bruce Springsteen country, then west along the legendary Route 66, stopping in town after town to show clothes at department stores during the day and do my act in clubs in the evening.

Many gullible Americans appeared to believe that my lordly status was real and time and again I was given a civic reception and treated like royalty. The British consular officials were remarkably supportive in helping me set up engagements, playing the game even though they knew I was not a proper lord.

I sold a lot of clothes, but got a clue to American tastes when I was unable to shift twelve heavy Sherlock Holmes coats in psychedelic tartans which I'd planned to unload the second I got to New York during their bitterly cold January. But no one showed any interest in them until I reached Los Angeles, when they were snapped up as just the gear for posing round Sunset Strip on mildly chilly evenings.

The crazy world of Los Angeles had always been my real goal rather than San Francisco, as I was not really into the hippy thing. When I went to Haight Ashbury I hated it but I happily settled into LA and soon made a new friend in Rodney Bingenheimer, who was a bit like me in being the self-styled 'Mayor of Sunset Strip'. Bingenheimer was a disc jockey, whose claim to fame was having been a stand-in for Davy Jones of the Monkees, whom he quite closely resembled. He was also a leading light on the party circuit, contributing gossip and a column to the *Los Angeles Times*.

I met Bingenheimer at the Whisky à Go Go on the Strip, where all the famous artists like Dylan and the Byrds had performed, and thanks to his social connections and English guests being all the rage, was soon attending top parties and seeing people like Charlton Heston, Fats Domino, Ray Charles, and Ike and Tina Turner. The highlight for me was having a long discussion with Edward G. Robinson, who by then was very old. He had the air of a man who had seen it all and, partly because he was smoking a cigar, looked very like Winston Churchill but I thought it better not to say anything for fear of being rubbed out.

From a Jack to a King

My greatest thrill of all was in 1969 when Elvis made his comeback. His series of concerts at the International Hotel in Las Vegas was an instant sell-out, but Rodney told me there was a special showing for two thousand members of the press. I rang for tickets, explaining I was the British Ambassador for Rock and Roll, and got them by return enabling me to attend the greatest performance I had ever seen. Elvis was at his best for those concerts, psyched up, hungry for success, and moving, singing and looking like a 100 per cent superstar. The first four numbers just swept by me as I was numbed by seeing him in the flesh after enduring hundreds of fake Elvises in Britain. But I soon calmed down and enjoyed the concert, joining in the rapturous applause as he did three encores.

Rodney and I had a brief chat with the King afterwards and got his autograph while I gave him Tom

Jones's regards and added my own voice to Tom's plea that he come across to England. Elvis replied he'd love to, but he had to ask both his manager and his father. And, he added, if he did come to England he would also have to visit the rest of Europe, and especially Spain, where there were tens of thousands of Elvis look-alikes.

Even as he spoke I knew he would never make it.

Putting on the Style

While I was in America England with its petty troubles seemed worlds away, until I received an urgent request from my friends in Carnaby Street. Although the street was still the centre of the universe, the shopkeepers were having great difficulty because of the traffic which clogged it up and spoilt the atmosphere. Sensibly, they wanted it to be turned into a pedestrian precinct and knowing my political credentials pleaded with me to stand in the 1970 General Election to get something done. I agreed, and as my National Teenage party had been made redundant by Harold, chose the title of the Go To Blazes party – a variation on my original political idea of the Sod 'Em All party.

I ran a colourful and carefree campaign in the street's best tradition, using the opportunity to show off my varied wardrobe in its true surroundings. Eventually our cause won through and the street was pedestrian-ized but at the time, as soon as I'd done the business, I saw no reason to stay in Britain and returned to my new life in America.

He Ain't Heavy, He's Your Brother

Back in LA I fully experienced the positive American attitude toward getting things done. In all the years I had made singles I had never got round to cutting an album. But when all my old mates who were now with big-name bands started rolling into LA I saw my opportunity.

There were the Moody Blues, whose links with me went back to their early days when they had been my support in Birmingham. Also Led Zeppelin and the Rolling Stones, whose musicians such as John Bonham and Jimmy Page offered to come and play on the album I had started recording. Deep Purple arrived with Nicky Simper and Ritchie Blackmore, who told me it had been more exciting playing with the Savages, where they had eyeball-to-eyeball contact with the audience, than the vast American stadiums where they could see nothing but darkness. Deep Purple was playing at a private party being thrown by the *Playboy* boss Hugh Hefner and they invited me along, warning me there was a strict instruction not to bring any girls. I could see why when we got there – it made the Miss World contest look like a Wimpy Bar.

The only snag with making the album was not having the cash to pay for the recording sessions upfront. This would have been a huge problem in Britain, but the American answer was to tell me I could pay the bills after the record had been released and made some money – which I subsequently did. The album was called *Lord Sutch and His Heavy Friends*, and it also featured my ex-Savages of Jeff Beck, Noel Redding and Nicky Hopkins. It was my greatest success, rising to

Number 48 in the American Billboard charts. I followed it up with another LP of live gigs called *Hands of Jack the Ripper*, which was released in 1972 to tie in with a rock and roll extravaganza at Wembley Stadium.

Shake Rattle and Roll

I flew back to join the bill for this show at Wembley in 1972, which was the greatest line-up of rock and rollers ever seen in this country – Little Richard, Jerry Lee Lewis, Chuck Berry, Bo Diddley, Gary Glitter, Bill Haley and the Comets, the Move, the Platters, the Drifters, the Coasters, Billy Fury and me.

Backstage, bumping into all these legends, it was like opening a door and being confronted by a sea of faces you'd known all your life. By then Bill Haley was 47, but he was still knocking out 'Rock Around the Clock'. 'I'll always be grateful to you for putting me on the right road with the Winston Churchill business back in the '50s,' I told him when we had the chance for a quick word.

'One, two, three o'clock, four o'clock, rock . . .' Haley replied with a dazed look. Instantly I saw that by now he had been completely zombified by the tens of thousands of times he'd sung the song and there seemed little point in continuing the conversation.

'See you later, alligator,' I told him.

'In a while, crocodile,' he replied and we left it at that.

There was a lot of nervousness beforehand as this was the first time Wembley had been used for a pop concert. But it was a perfect August day and the stadium was filled to its capacity of 100,000 – the biggest audience I ever played. After that I never felt frightened in front of a crowd again. The concert marked the end of an era and I celebrated with an extra-special performance, with the coffin carried on by some skimpily clad ladies. But I had to keep that part quite tame as the management was frightened of me going over the top as usual and warned me they would pull the plug on the whole show if the girls stripped off beyond a certain point.

Bachelor Boy

There was a good reason for their concern. Just before the concert I had caused quite a stir when I realized that despite all the efforts to make this the best line-up ever, one extremely important artist was missing – Ted Heath and his Band. After the 1970 election I had been happy to relax in LA, knowing shiftly old Harold had been replaced as Prime Minister by Ted Heath. The Big Band sound, with lots of brass, was what I felt the country needed and all reports said Ted was touring successfully and pulling good houses all over the country.

For the concert I'd implored Ted to play with the backing of the full band to give Little Richard something really to worry about. But he'd been very stuffy about the whole thing and told me pompously a carol concert at Broadstairs was much more his line. In a last-ditch effort to persuade him, or at least give him some free tickets so he could join the audience as a guest celeb, I took some naked girls to Downing Street to show him what he would be missing.

We got almost to the door of Number 10 before the

police stepped in and arrested us, taking off their helmets to place them strategically in front of the girls' private parts. I was fully dressed by my standards in my leopardskin leotard, but I was still charged with insulting behaviour. It hadn't occurred to me at the time, but I realized afterwards that my main crime had actually been frightening the life out of Heath, whom I had seen peering round the edge of the net curtains at this terrifying display of female flesh. In court I put up a sterling defence and was acquitted, but the girls, unable to produce a shred of evidence as a cover story, were fined £20 each. I paid this on their behalf by selling off the tickets I had intended to give Ted.

I think it was the shock of this incident that caused Heath to start rapidly going downhill. His failure to show at Wembley led to his street cred plummeting and in desperation he tried to expand the Band's horizons by joining the European Musicians' Community. But the fans were only lukewarm and when he cut his gigs down to a three-day week and put all the lights out even the diehards had had enough. In the 1974 election the country finally ditched him.

I agreed with the majority that the old bachelor should chuck the Band and go off to play his organ solo. But of course the result was we got Wilson back, as slimy and devious as ever. In the election I did not stand against him, but instead put myself up at Stafford and Stone, where I was playing a nightclub in a stately home. My platform of the Ban the Old Fogeys party indicated how bored I was with the whole scene. Really I was just keeping my hand in, and I switched off even more as Harold tried to suck up to the unions before giving up and handing over to

Jim Callaghan. Callaghan in turn I never rated, seeing him as a real middle-of-the-roader – a Des O'Connor of politics appealing to a similarly vacuous audience – who got the comeuppance that he deserved when he bombed with his Winter of Discontent.

HOMEWARD BOUND

DURING THE dreary decade of the '70s I alternated between Britain and America, with a bias to being over on the States' side. In LA I found a handy apartment off Sunset Boulevard with a pool and a safe lock-up round the back for the Roller. I had regular work playing the top clubs like the Whisky à Go Go and the Troubador in Santa Monica, a favourite venue for bands like the Grateful Dead and where Jim Morrison and the Doors got their big break.

More importantly for me Rodney Bingenheimer introduced me to Thann Rendessy, who became my wife. Thann was one of LA's top models, with a soft oval face and high cheekbones which I thought made her look like an angel, and the most perfect figure I had ever seen. At first Thann had a lot of trouble understanding my English accent, while I had equal difficulty with her Texan drawl, but we warmed to each other immediately. As we got to know each other I was delighted to discover she was not just a dumb blonde but highly intelligent, with a good sense of humour and a great interest in music.

Thann moved in within a week and we soon established a fun outdoors life, spending a lot of time at parties on the beach, where she also taught me to surf. Through her I was able to see a lot of the weird life of LA, while she enjoyed my gigs. Our relationship was given an extra spice by the clash of cultures between Britain and America and I found myself relaxing into the LA lifestyle as I absorbed her laidback attitude.

Thann came across to England with me and in 1975 we had a son, who was born in Northwick Park hospital in Watford Road, Harrow. I was thrilled and wanted to call him Screaming Lord Sutch, but Thann objected and insisted he be called Tristan. So he ended up as Tristan Lord Sutch.

Riders On the Storm

Politically the '70s were my wilderness years, and knocking around with people like Jim Morrison of the Doors, I found most American musicians had even stronger views on politicians than those in Britain. When I got to LA I used to go clubbing with Jim, although I couldn't keep up with him as he was so totally gross. By then he was so fed up with being mobbed he had let himself go to seed, growing a huge black beard to destroy his pretty boy image and finally dressing in scruffy clothes so he just looked like a bad-tempered, smelly hippy.

Morrison told me he hated politicians for taking his tax money and wasting it on bombs. They were all a load of corrupt bastards, he said, and fuck 'em all. Like many of the musicians I met in America he regarded his work as the music of anti-politics.

I saw what he meant when Tricky Dicky Nixon went over Watergate, to be succeeded first by Gerald Ford and then Jimmy Carter. Neither of these interested me much, as they were obviously country and western fans. But in LA I ran into a local Californian politician,

Ronnie Reagan, who was rising fast and being tipped for the top, and thanks to the social circuit I was on with Bingenheimer I was able to meet him after he saw my Union Jack Roller and told a friend of Rodney's he'd like to meet the owner.

I was invited to one of the dos at his ranch, where I was greeted at the gate by Nancy, who immediately asked me what sign I was born under. I replied: 'Please keep off the grass,' and for a moment she looked mystified before clutching me warmly by the arm. 'Oh Your Highness-ship,' she gushed, 'I do so admire you young people who are joining our fight against the evils of drugs. Now you just keep up the good work!'

In a way I have. Although I've tried my share of heavy drinking of various sorts and used to smoke cigarettes, I've always kept away from serious drugs and alcohol. It's not that I don't enjoy drinking, but it gives me migraine headaches and instead I've always been a prolific tea-drinker – a habit I think I picked up from Mum. There's another reason as well. People often think wild performers must be completely out of their heads all the time, but the truth is the really crazy acts, like mine, Alice Cooper, Ozzie Osbourne of Black Sabbath, and Arthur Brown who followed me, are very dangerous and require a cool head and razor-sharp reactions if they are to be kept under control.

Da-Doo-Ron-Ron-Ron, Da-Doo-Ron-Ron

I was explaining all this to Nancy, and how I'd been involved in British politics and stood for Parliament several times, when she interrupted me to say I must

meet her husband, who we found practising his putting near the pool. 'Now then, Ronnie,' she told him,
'this is David Sutch, the owner of that Rolls-Royce you
saw the other day. And fancy, it turns out he's not only
an English lord but one of their leading politicians!'

'Shoot!' replied Reagan, holding out a paper bag
and offering me a jelly baby.' So you're in the movie
business too, are you, your Lordliness? Well, it sure is
a privilege to meet a Brit star of the silver screen.'

As he started rattling on about his old films and
how wonderful Hollywood was I tried to break in to
tell him I was not an actor, but a singer, and what I
really wanted to talk to him about was politics.

'I've stood for Parliament several times,' I finally
managed to inform him when he broke off to pick
up a net and start fishing misdirected golf balls out
of the pool.

Reagan suddenly looked puzzled and I saw his brow
furrow with concentration. 'I don't think I've ever
heard of that Parliament movie,' he finally replied
slowly. 'It can't have been a Western, or I'd know it.'
Then his face suddenly brightened up. 'Oh, I get it,' he
said. 'It must be your Brit way of saying Paramount –
great studio, son, but you're right – one of the hardest
to get into.'

I was about to try explaining again when Nancy
came bustling up. 'Now then, Ronnie,' she chided
him. 'I can see you've gotten stuck into politics, but
I've just noticed Venus is in the ascendant, so it's time
for you to come down on me!'

Reagan gave me a goofy grin as he allowed himself
to be led away, adding: 'Well, son, if there's anything
I can do for you, just let me know. I'll have plenty
of influence in Paramount when I get to these White

House studios I've signed for. After all, we movie stars must stick together, eh?'

Dazed by all this, I consulted Rodney and my other music mates, who howled with laughter when I recounted the conversation. Reagan, they explained, had been carefully selected for the new age of TV entertainment scheduled to supersede politics in America.

'Go and see some of his old films,' they advised. 'Then you'll see what's coming for all of us.'

I hunted down a few in backstreet cinemas and was astonished to see what crappy B-movies they were. But when I protested to my mates that they must have meant another actor, they just laughed even more. 'You don't think they'd choose a good actor, do you?' they replied, explaining that Reagan had been specifically chosen as such a ham that in one of his films he had been out-acted by a chimpanzee. Anyone with class, like Dustin Hoffman, Robert de Niro or Donald Duck, they told me, would have been accused of over-acting the way he carried on.

Working-Class Hero

Although I was still enjoying meeting oddballs like Reagan, who so personified the Hollywood attitude, America had its downside. It was the violence which got to me in the end and I never really recovered from the shock of the murder of John Lennon. I'd done the Toronto Rock and Roll Festival in Maple Leaf Gardens with him, when we'd been the only two English singers on a bill topped by Jim Morrison and the Doors.

John had been in a sombre mood and with his

beard and the white suit he looked and sounded more like a preacher than a singer. He told me was fed up with being interrogated about what direction he was going in and the endless analysis of his music. He just wanted to get back to his roots of rock and roll standards, which was why he had formed the Plastic Ono band with Eric Clapton, who he rated highly, on lead guitar. John's biggest kick at the concert had been meeting his idol Gene Vincent for the first time since years earlier at the Star Club in Hamburg, when Gene had been an international star and the Beatles were virtually unknown.

Whilst I carried on my flirtation with America during the '70s, it led me into more petty troubles than John's. The safe lock-up did not save my beloved Roller, which was stolen and never recovered despite being so distinctive and my offering a $10,000 reward, but that was minor compared to the nasty experience I had in New York. Late one night I made the classic mistake of getting on a subway train going the wrong way and I got out at a station in the middle of Harlem clutching a briefcase and wearing trendy clothes. I had only gone a few yards when a young black jumped out of a shop doorway, aimed a gun at me and shouted: 'Give me your fucking wallet and your money.'

As I froze and went dry in the mouth he glared at me and then pulled the trigger. There was the loudest bang I've ever heard in my life and I felt myself go numb. I dropped the briefcase to check I was still there and when I got my senses back and looked round he had gone. Eventually I stood right in front of a cab to make it stop and got back to my hotel and to this day I don't know whether the gun contained a blank or whether he just missed. Maybe, some wag suggested afterwards, he had just been too poor to buy any bullets.

We Shall Not Be Moved

I had also experienced violence at pop concerts, and even in the park near my apartment, where there were frequent flare-ups between the police sneering at young people sitting around, calling them hippy scum, whilst the people shouted back that cops were fascists. The police would then move in and before you knew what was happening the batons would be brought out and shots fired in the air, so that what had started as a little acoustic guitar playing quickly escalated into a violent madhouse.

These incidents usually sprang up as a result of protests about Vietnam, which was an issue I did not really feel part of. But I was saddened by the vets who would go on stage at pop concerts and anti-war rallies to explain how their lives had been destroyed by the war, through either terrible physical injuries or mental and emotional damage. However, the anti-war movement was not universally popular and at pop concerts the audience would often get bored and shout at the performers to stop preaching and get on with the music. Then more flare-ups would start.

But the incident which personally upset me most was at the liquor store just up the road from our apartment. This had an automatic alarm that linked the store to the police station and when it went off one evening the cops roared up to challenge two guys they could see inside holding armfuls of booze and cigarettes. When one of them went to open a drawer, the police shot him dead. The next day it came out that the dead man was the son of the owner who had gone to the store to get more drink and cigarettes for a party. He had accidentally set the alarm off letting himself in and when he was shot he had been going to the drawer to get his bunch of keys to switch it off.

Happening just on my doorstep, this made me sick to my stomach and I thanked God British coppers weren't tooled up like that, in a country where a life can be snuffed out over a few bottles of booze and packets of fags.

The Dark Side of the Moon

There were other more publicized deaths which affected me as well, particularly that of Elvis. Like millions of others I sadly watched his steep decline until he finally died, bloated and wrecked by drugs, in 1977. I was playing in Germany when the news broke and at first didn't believe it as I can't read German and couldn't understand the details in the papers. But when it did sink in I joined the awful sense of loss for a man who had given so much pleasure and hope to so many people before he himself became a victim of the American dream.

The music business encourages people to excess, and Elvis was only one of the many who died who meant something to me. But of all the fellow musicians who fell by the way, I think the one I was saddest about was Keith Moon. I went to see Keith in the mid '70s at his futuristic house in Chertsey, Surrey. It had a long driveway with cars strewn along both sides of it – old Buicks and Mercs and all sorts of exotic machinery. In the middle of them all stood a milk float. Keith never got a full driving licence, probably because he was always too drunk to pass his test, but he had found out from the milkman that you didn't need one to drive a float. He promptly bought one from the dairy by making them an offer they could not refuse and used it to go to the pub and get as pissed as he liked without the police being able to do anything about it.

And although he didn't take the cars on to the road, he used to career up and down the drive knocking them into each other like big bumper cars. It was all part of his attitude that life was one big joke, and he refused to take it seriously or think about the value of anything. I ended up staying with him for three days, going out with him on mad manoeuvres and pub crawls where he got pissed and tried to freak people out by sending them up and talking to them in funny accents.

For one night on the town he dressed up as a member of the German Gestapo, complete with swastikas. But Keith always went too far, even for me, and I finally baled out at 9 a.m. when he ordered the driver to take him to Golders Green so he could go round upsetting the Jewish shopkeepers. It was obvious then he would burn himself out. He wasn't known as 'Moon the Loon' for nothing, but he was a smashing bloke and I loved him dearly.

Why Do Fools Fall in Love?

Towards the end of the '70s I was increasingly drawn back to Britain. Thann suffered badly from post-natal depression and did not like the food or the weather here, and she finally went back to America with

Tristan. We have stayed good friends in the years since the separation, though I was devastated by her leaving, and whilst I felt I could not go back to America permanently, I have made many trips back there. By the beginning of the '80s I was fully resident in Britain.

In August 1976 I met Giselle Menhenett, a bubbly French blonde who lived in Paris and London. Giselle was a costume jewellery designer and antique collector and we fell in love almost immediately and she has now been my beloved partner for many years and accompanied me on a number of my American trips. As a special present for my birthday soon after we met she bought me the mock leopardskin jacket from Caroline Walker in Kensington Market which later became my political uniform.

Giselle lived in a Victorian terrace house near Portobello Road, beautifully furnished in her own flamboyant style with a mixture of French art nouveau and English period furniture, so we referred to my house White Lodge in Harrow as our 'country house' until I sold it. Tristan came across to live with us for a number of years and proved to be a chip off the old block by giving an imitation of my stage show at the age of three.

Giselle and I have a happy relationship, sharing tastes in music and films as well as both being collectors, and she has a hearty Gallic contempt for all politicians which I much admire. She is now in charge of my props department, but otherwise stays well away from British politics – although she has always told me she can't wait until we get to Number 10 so that she can redesign the interior and make it a bit more exciting!

Anarchy in the UK

Drifting more and more away from America I found the English music scene redeveloping after the years of sterility in the early '70s. In 1977, the year of the Queen's Silver Jubilee, Malcolm MacLaren had started the Sex Pistols, establishing a new formula of hype and outrage which caused just as much fuss as I had at the beginning of the '60s.

I had known Malcolm for years, and he had made my original teddy boy outfits, but I still found it hard to believe what he had got going. The Sex Pistols were horrible and the noise they made sounded like a music shop on a Saturday morning when everybody was trying out different instruments. But the hype worked. Thousands were inspired to believe – quite rightly – that they could make just as good a sound, and some did better, like the Stranglers, the Clash and the Damned. But one way or another they were all giving voice to a new, raucous Britain very different from the peace and love of the '60s.

MacLaren was the king of hype, but he did have a point in saying that the top groups had got too smooth and out of touch. The Jubilee celebrations, aimed at the new core audience of visiting American tourists, seemed hopelessly old fashioned in comparison whilst the BBC, as always, toed the line and sided with the Establishment by banning the Sex Pistols' record 'God Save the Queen'.

What I soon realized when I was re-established back in Britain and the '80s dawned was that the same thing had been happening on the political scene as had taken place in rock. After Maggie had been elected as Conservative leader in 1975 the Tory line-up had changed from the easy listenin' of the Ted Heath Band to prototype heavy metal. The new top group was now the Iron Lady, with a line-up of heavies ranging from the Chingford Skinhead Norman Tebbitt on drums, to the Mad Monk Sir Keith Joseph on lead guitar. When I called my booking agency of Sutchy and Sutchy they explained that Maggie and the Tories had been revamped by some obscure ad agency for the new era of the '80s that we were now entering.

Leader of the Pack

However, my interest in Thatcher was only slight until I personally experienced the violence of the new Britain. I'd always felt safe on the London streets, so perhaps it was my fault for not taking precautions, but as I was walking through the Portobello Road market in the early hours one morning I was set upon from behind and mugged. I never saw my assailants, as I blacked out from a nasty crack on the head, and I came round to find myself lying in the gutter. Staring at me was the headline of a newspaper which had been chucked into the road beside me: GANG OF FOUR LAUNCHES NEW BATTLE OF BRITAIN! it screamed.

As the words swam in front of me I felt a sharp, throbbing pain in my hand. Immediately my mind flashed back to my Kilburn childhood and I saw once again the great bulbous face of my Mentor, Winston Churchill, looming above me. 'For Sutch is the way it is; and Sutch therefore is the way it will always be,' his voice boomed and a series of visions rapidly flashed in front of my eyes – the Punch I had carved, Bill Haley, my by-election triumphs, the cigar I had been handed by the Tory agent at Huyton – all the signals of my chosen destiny which had somehow slipped from my mind during my wilderness years, and which even meeting Ronnie Reagan had failed to trigger off.

Gingerly getting to my feet, I picked up the newspaper and staggered home to read about these new political usurpers of the crown Winston had handed me, my voting hand on fire with pain – just as it had when the greatest Englishman of our times had first marked me out as his natural successor. Now that my eyes had been re-opened, the vision before me chilled me to the bone.

Red Red Wine

Thatcher was miles away from Winston and obviously was much too wild to be a true representative of the people. On the other side of the political fence things were just as demented, with old Michael Foot, the original Man in a Grey Duffel Coat, successfully taking the Labour party back fifty years. It was in the middle, however, that there was real trouble, as the newspapers trumpeted the successes of the Gang of Four.

I thought the name a poor one for a band – if their aim was government the Four Tops would have been better – and by now most people will have forgotten the names of the original line-up – Roy Rogers, an old movie-star crony of Reagan's riding on the back of Trigger; Woy Jenkins, a wine trade rep specializing in claret who was just back from a spell in the Brussels office; Shirley Williams, a part-time housewife; and the man who was to become my most bitter enemy of all of them – the former mortuary attendant, Dr 'Death' Owen.

The Gang of Four's first album, the Social Democratic party, had been an instant hit and even got Woy Jenkins back into Parliament, despite the cruelty of putting him up as candidate in Wawwington, where the wodka comes from. But worst of all the Gang was now claiming my Winston mantle of representing the people by claiming they were giving a voice to the silent majority. I thought this a brilliant ploy as being silent, this 'majority' was hardly likely to speak up to deny it and when I examined the members of the group individually, of all four it was David Owen who needled me most. Owen had once been a charismatic figure on the political scene, Foreign Secretary in the Labour government at the age of only thirty-eight, and named Britain's sexiest politician by that giant of political opinion, the *Daily Express*.

The political world had appeared to be at his feet, with women voters swooning at his boyish smile and buccaneering attitude. But in other fields he had not been so popular, and he was known in the Commons as an arrogant, prickly character. Labour might have been a sick party needing a doctor, but that hadn't prevented him falling out with his old comrades and walking out in a huff.

Well, Goodness Gracious Me!

The SDP Gang had kicked off with the Limehouse Declaration, a pompous document named after Owen's magnificent house in the East End where the original meeting had been held to put the group together. As the house fronted directly on to the river I decided to use this watery avenue to drop in and find out more about what was going on.

I borrowed a small boat and approached to see Owen on the balcony, playing the French game of boules with his wife Deborah, who incidentally was Jeffrey Archer's literary agent.

'Yo ho ho!' I cried matily, waving my bottle of rum and adjusting the parrot on my shoulder. 'Avast there, me hearties! Shiver me timbers, for the sun is over the yardarm and methinks 'tis time for our daily tot o'grog!'

Owen looked up in horror. 'Stand by to repel boarders!' he yelled, gesticulating frantically to keep me away. 'Entry strictly limited to invitation and credit card!'

I cursed myself for forgetting to carry the key document of a copy of the *Guardian* to signal I was a PLU (People Like Us), which I now realized would have been my ticket to land.

'How about some grog?' I hollered back, hoping this would crack the equation, but Owen looked even more horrified.

'Proved beyond doubt!' he shrieked. 'Only claret and red wine drinkers allowed on board. Be gone, scurvy prole, before I set our new community police on you!'

Seeing I could make no headway, I allowed the boat to start drifting back into midstream, until the parrot fortunately helped retrieve the situation for me.

'Who's a pretty boy, then!' it squawked, and Owen

instantly dashed his hand through his thick black hair as he automatically snapped into photo-opportunity mode.

Vanity, I instantly saw, could be his undoing in the end.

WALKIN' BACK TO
HAPPINESS

CHIPPENHAM MEWS in Paddington is at first sight as
unprepossessing as the area round Dr Owen's Limehouse mansion. At a casual glance it appears to be
a grubby alley of the sort that might be inhabited
by ladies of the night. But it was here, in a humble
flat over a garage, that Winston's Inheritance finally
blossomed.

After the formation of the SDP Gang and my brush
with Dr Owen I felt more and more isolated. My old
enemy Harold Wilson had disappeared to the Scilly
Isles where he obviously belonged, and my old band
members, my Ambassadors of Rock, had scattered to
the four corners of the Earth. It was Pauline Healy, an
old friend in the music business, who put me back
on track. One evening, after I had dropped in for a
cup of tea at her flat, I was unable to contain myself
any longer. As I told her about my bump on the head
and how it had restored the memory of the Winston
Inheritance, I felt a great lightening of my spirit at
sharing my burden. Pauline examined the scar on
my hand and her eyes sparkled with indignation as
I explained how the smooth-talking Gang of Four was
seeking to delude my faithful but often gullible people
with their Volvo-led 'social democracy'.

When I reached the end of my melancholy tale I
took a sup of tea and fell silent. For a time Pauline too

said nothing as she gazed pensively into the flickering depths of the log-effect fire. Eventually she broke the long silence. 'Well, David, what are you going to do about these people?' she asked.

Suddenly I heard a growling voice in my ears and saw Pauline staring at me open-mouthed. 'We shall fight on the beaches,' I heard myself saying in an unaccustomedly gruff voice, 'we shall fight on the landing grounds, we shall fight in the fields and in the streets, we shall fight on the hills. We shall never surrender.'

The next day we sent out our first press release. The Official Monster Raving Loony party had been formed – with plenty of common sense behind the choice of name:

* Official – No other party in Britain has the word Official in its name, so all the other parties are therefore unofficial.
* Monster – I had a monster act and there was nothing more monstrous than politicians.
* Raving – All politicians rave and I'd been a raver for years.
* Loony – Everybody had told me I was a real Loony standing for Parliament

Whilst we were at it we adopted the Loch Ness Monster as the party mascot on the grounds that it inhabited deep and murky waters, refused all photo-opportunities, and did not speak to the press. It has promised to surface when I am made Prime Minister. Finally, I decided that if I was going to be a Raving Loony I should dress as one. This time there would be no top hat and tails, or advice from shifty Harold.

Instead I would stand in the leopardskin jacket Giselle had given me, while the party as such would adopt yellow.

Born in the USA

Glancing across the pond I saw another event propelling me back into politics. The movie-star politician I had met, Ronnie Reagan, was now proudly hamming it up as President as my mates had predicted. I quickly scoured the new video rental shops to complete my master collection of his old movies. When I compared them to his presidential TV performances I was delighted to see that Ronnie had kept up his low acting standards and it was obvious the Americans loved him as much as ET, who I thought might have been modelled on his wrinkly appearance.

And as the posters showed, his effect on Maggie was even more electric. It was indeed a masterly remake of *Gone With the Wind* as Good Ole Ronnie swept her off her feet. Bearing in mind what he had said at his ranch, to prepare for my political comeback I quickly moved to neutralize any trans-Atlantic challenge by him through signing our historic SALT (Stop All Transmissions) Agreement. Under this Reagan promised not to make any more films, whilst I agreed not to make any more records. I will always be grateful to him for not breaking it.

Waterloo Sunset

I decided to begin my comeback early in 1983 with the by-election at Bermondsey, the constituency which covers the area round the Elephant and Castle and Waterloo station. Bermondsey is a typical rundown inner-city area and had always been Labour until that time, but it was then at the centre of a major row inside the party. The old right-wing MP Bob Mellish had resigned from the local party because of the direction it was taking and the new candidate, Peter Tatchell, was being panned in the press as a member of the Loony Left.

When I went to register as a candidate I found the by-election was also setting a new record by having a total of sixteen candidates on the ballot paper, which as a result was fifteen inches long. This followed the pattern of the last few years with an increasing number of fringe candidates, with nine in one constituency in the 1979 General Election, rising to twelve at Croydon in 1981. Knowing the competition was fearsome, and being so rusty after my wilderness years, I found campaigning in the bitter January and February weather hard going. But fate had obviously had a hand in bringing me back, for at the count I met the man who came to influence me more than anyone since Winston – the late Commander Bill Boaks.

King of the Road

In all my years as a candidate Boaks had been at the back of my mind. Although I had made my mark by the novel ploy of being a totally honest politician, on this front he towered above even me.

Lieutenant-Commander Boaks had gone into politics in the early '50s after fighting a distinguished war in the service of the Navy, for whom he had been a gunnery officer on HMS *Rodney* at the sinking of the *Bismarck*. He stood as Public Safety Democratic Monarchist White Resident candidate. He never tried to expand into a party but instead repeatedly stood in elections and by-elections, starting in 1951 and contesting so many that in the end even he couldn't remember how many there had been. He thought it was about thirty, which is easily possible because in general elections he took advantage of the rules to put himself up in three or four constituencies at once, which is perfectly legal as long as he paid the necessary deposits.

Boaks's main platform and preoccupation was the issue of road safety. His brilliant solution to the problem was that every road in Britain should be made a zebra crossing unless marked otherwise. This would mean that, apart from the narrow strips of existing crossings, pedestrians would have precedence over vehicles everywhere. What struck me as amazing about this policy was its glorious simplicity: there would be no need to modify existing roads or signs to implement it, and although it would obviously cause chaos, it was impossible to deny Boaks's contention that it would save lives.

I also admired the way the Commander was determined to prove his point about danger on the roads. He hated cars so much that he regularly loaded an old pram with house bricks and then went out on to the streets in Streatham, where he lived. Positioning himself at a zebra crossing he would wait until an oncoming car was an inch away, and then shove the pram into its path. Just to ram his point home, he also formed the habit of regularly standing in the fast lane of the Kingston by-pass wearing his woolly bobble hat and ostentatiously reading the *Daily Telegraph*.

CC Rider

On the night of the count at Bermondsey I was called out of the town hall and told that Boaks had arrived but that he was having trouble getting in because, for once, he was not a candidate in the election. His antics on the road had finally got him into trouble and he was still recovering from a serious collision with a motorcycle.

I went outside to meet him thinking this legendary figure would be very smart with lots of money, but instead I found a little old guy in a tweed jacket who looked like a poor farm worker and very, very old fashioned. He reminded me of my old agent Reg Calvert in his 'country dress' days. We were introduced and I could tell he was really shocked by my Loony leopardskin jacket and red top hat.

'You must certainly get noticed in that outfit,' he remarked after a long pause.

As I was wearing a saucer-sized, fluorescent yellow and black Loony badge I quickly replied: 'Yes, it's brilliant for road safety. With this stuff on, I always feel safe on the roads.'

The remark obviously endeared me to him, and he warmed to me further when I ran him through brief details of my Carnaby Street pedestrianization campaign. Relaxed, he now showed me his campaign vehicle, which he had brought with him. I had heard tales of this legendary machine, an armoured adult tricycle which he had built himself from bits and pieces including part of an iron bedstead. It weighed, he told me, fully 200 pounds, and it was embellished with large pieces of cardboard bearing his election slogans and press cuttings about road accidents and juggernauts crushing little villages. I had heard Boaks used this alarming vehicle for campaigning, but because he was so strapped for funds he also travelled on it to the constituency where the by-election was being held.

The story ran that he would set off as soon as the election was announced, but as he was already in late middle age when he had started in politics he was only able to pedal this heavyweight contraption about fifteen miles a day. If the constituency was far away he would sometimes not arrive until the campaign was over, thereby making no speeches whatsoever and meeting no one. When I mentioned this he agreed he had experienced difficulties, but explained the tricycle was central to his campaigning style. He was usually ignored if he just stood on the pavement, so he always parked it across pedestrian crossings, thereby blocking the traffic and providing himself with a captive audience.

Most ironic of all, although I was too polite to mention it, was the well-known fact that the large pieces of cardboard made his juggernaut one of the most dangerous vehicles on the road, as it was peculiarly vulnerable to side winds and a sudden gust could send it veering uncontrollably into the path of oncoming traffic.

Silence Is Golden

To solve Boaks's problem of how to get into the town hall I offered to make him one of my counting agents and had a pass made out in his name. Once inside he then repaid me by racing around like a mountain goat on my behalf, puffing and panting and telling me how you had to watch these buggers as they sometimes put your votes on the Labour piles. As he darted about, holding an armful of papers on which he made copious notes, I was irresistibly reminded of an elderly Apache circling the wagons, except he was firing glares instead of arrows at the counters.

At that point the Commander had just achieved a record with an all-time low of only five votes in the by-election at Glasgow Hillhead. Under the electoral rules you need the signatures of ten voters in the constituency to stand, so this was quite an achievement. Apart from the fact that nobody else had been interested in his policies, at least half the people who had nominated him had then not even bothered to vote for him. Asked afterwards why he thought he had done so badly, he had replied: 'The Scots are always known as a mean people. Now it seems they're mean with their votes too.'

I inquired what he thought of this new-found fame and to my surprise he answered: 'I've never cared whether anybody votes for me or not. Most voters are like sheep, you know. They just put their cross against Labour or Conservative because that's what they've always done. They don't actually think. The people who really count are the ones who don't vote.

It's their vote I want because they're the only ones with the sense to see through it all.'

This intrigued me, as it applied to all my rock and roll mates and most of the people I knew. 'Tell me more,' I encouraged him.

'It's these people, the non-voters, who I stand for,' he explained. 'And if you study election results like I have, you'll find time and again that the number of people not voting is greater than the number voting for the so-called winner.'

I knew this was true in Britain, and even truer in the USA, where less than half the population had voted for anyone in the Presidential election, never mind Ronnie Reagan who supposedly 'won'. In Boaks's case, however, there was a different point.

'But why stand in so many elections if you're not interested in getting any votes?' I asked him.

'There's a simple answer to that,' he replied slightly wearily, as though he had been asked this question many times before. 'I represent the non-voters who practically always win. It's unofficial, of course, because the Establishment pretends not to notice, but in my book it means I can't lose. And that's why I like standing. You see, I always know beforehand that unofficially I'm going to be on the winning side!'

Eye of the Tiger

I was just trying to sort this out in my head when Boaks broke off to demand one of my manifestos. He appeared baffled by my policy of erecting a statue to Tommy Steele – the Bermondsey Bombshell and only decent thing ever to come out of the place. But he still took a copy and said he would add it to his filing system, which he told me filled every room in his house from floor to ceiling, mostly with newspaper cuttings about road accidents, careless and drunken drivers, and damage caused by heavy lorries.

Then he suddenly delved into his mound of papers, thrusting aside several copies of the Highway Code, and pulled out a grubby exercise book, curled at the edges and covered in tea stains. Across the cover was crudely typed: 'How to Survive in Politics Without Getting Run Over'.

'It's all in here,' he started babbling at me. 'Lorries, lorries, everywhere, and not a soul will think . . .'

He fixed me with a gimlet eye, grabbed me by the arm as he brandished the book under my nose, and read:

> The time has come
> To talk of many things –
> Of cars and votes and accidents,
> Of people and of things,
> And why the roads are choc-a-bloc,
> And whether pigs have wings . . .
> 'Twas brillig, and the slimy cars
> Did gyre and gimble on the verge,
> All squashéd were pedestrians,
> The traffic we must purge!

Boaks made a wild sweeping gesture round the teeming hall. 'Look around you!' he cried. 'Regard these political types and see for yourself. Yea, slimy things do indeed crawl on slimy legs, here in Bermondsey!'

By now he was beginning to attract attention and I saw the police inspector in charge walking over to us.

'I wonder if you'd mind coming with me for a moment, sir?' he asked. I waited for Boaksy to be taken away, until I realized he was addressing me.

'Certainly, officer,' I replied, stepping forward.

Only a Pawn in the Game

What followed was a demonstration of how the Loony party is the party for law and order. Because of the heated atmosphere there were a lot of police around and, I was told, even armed police. I had already given the inspector a badge and manifesto so as to be on the right side of the law and now I listened to him maneouvring his men over the walkie-talkie as if they were in combat.

'This place is like a time bomb with the National Front and the Communists raring to have a go at each other,' he told me, going on to explain how I could help and save him, as he put it, 'opening another box of coppers'. Would I assemble my brightly coloured followers between the National Front and the rest as a buffer to keep them apart? he asked. In return we would be allowed to make as much noise as we liked.

My merry throng with their saucepan-sized rosettes and multiple badges thought this a brilliant idea and I promptly marshalled them into place. For the rest of the count the most effective policemen were therefore a wild crowd of Loonies, including a person in a clown's outfit, a Charlie Chaplin look-alike, a couple of Keystone Cops using uniforms from my stage show, and a man in a dustman's outfit.

As a clincher for the deal I obtained licence to wander about wherever I wanted without the police stopping me. This amazed Boaks and, when I returned to the area he was confined to, he grabbed me with his skinny hand.

'Now I can see that, like me, you have the gift,' he gabbled excitedly. 'You haven't got a tricycle, have you? I must tell you what lies ahead on the road we shall now pedal together . . . It's all in here!'

Waving 'How to Survive in Politics Without Being Run Over' at me, he started turning the pages, which I could see were lined and covered with close-packed spidery handwriting in different coloured inks. As he flipped through he read out snippets at random: 'Never time your election visits to people's houses so they coincide with popular TV programmes . . . Aristotle said: "Man is by nature a political animal."' He broke off and looked at me keenly with his blue sailor's eyes. 'You will notice Aristotle does not say man is a political motorist!' he added triumphantly.

'It's all in here!' he repeated feverishly as he thumbed through the pages. 'Everything you need to know to get nobody to vote for you! Just listen to this! "Pedestrians shall have right of way at all times, excepting when . . ."'

At that moment there was a huge roar from the National Front faction, where men in suits were orchestrating loud shouting and swearing by the skinhead element. Seeing that my followers were getting nervous at their unofficial policing role I hurriedly excused myself to go over and help. One thing led to another – as often happens with me – and somehow I never got back to Boaks. Perhaps if I had things might have turned out differently. But that night I little realized we were fated never to meet again, and the secrets in his book would remain with him for ever.

Red Sails in the Sunset

Although I'd been preoccupied with Boaks and the National Front drama, I hadn't been able to avoid noticing how the management of the election night at the town hall had become very American in style. Partly because TVam and Breakfast TV had just started up, there was now a plethora of cameras, which largely negated my old tactic of getting on the telly by homing in on the person being interviewed and hovering about, throwing in my own remarks. With four or five different camera crews it was difficult to know who to go for, so I made the wise choice of the Labour candidate Peter Tatchell, who was just about to bomb.

I told him I thought he'd got a bad deal from the press and how horrified I was that so much of the gentlemanliness seemed to have gone out of politics, both of which were true. What I didn't tell him was that he had been a disastrous candidate by anybody's standards and had really brought it on himself. Going round the markets I'd had people coming up to me, hyped up by the press and crucifying him for being an obnoxious Australian in the land of cockles and whelks and jellied eels. They kept accusing him of being gay, but the real problem was he was so hopelessly wet and fussy. He rode about on a sissy-looking bike with a wicker basket, and was preoccupied with holding meetings and issuing boring press statements rather then going out to meet people. So bad was he, even Michael Foot had disowned him as a candidate.

Mind you, Footy was still doing very badly himself, even though I'd bumped into him on Hampstead

Heath as he was exercising his little dog Dizzy and been so startled by his dishevelled appearance I'd felt it necessary to give him some advice. I'd strongly urged him to drop his duffel coat image in favour of a suit, but he had just glared at me and for a second I had thought he was going to hit me with the bound volume of Dick Crossman's speeches he was carrying. 'The people, the people, we must identify with the people,' he shouted at me, his grey hair blowing raggedly in the wind as he stomped off back to his huge Hampstead mansion, which was to be worth hundreds of thousands of pounds before the '80s were over.

The Bermondsey result was a disaster for Labour and more or less the final nail in its coffin before the General Election. But it gave fresh impetus to the Gang of Four, now teamed up with the Liberals, whose bright young candidate, Simon Hughes, who I found rather sweet, had won convincingly.

After all my efforts I was gutted at only getting 97 votes. But I knew I was out of practice and I had beaten ten other candidates, including, most impressively, the Communist party. Not only that, but my 97 votes had been more than both their wings put together. Communists have never been known for their sense of humour and I was bitterly attacked by comrades saying it was disgusting a Loony should get more votes than them. They were a legitimate party which had been going for years, they told me, yet the capitalist system had deluded the workers into giving their votes to a person wearing a dopey leopardskin outfit and a silly hat.

'I'm the Official Raving Loony candidate,' I eventually told some bearded dickhead when my patience had run out, 'so being a fool is something I should

Result of Bermondsey By-Election, 25 February 1983

No Vote	21,581
Simon Hughes (Liberal-SDP Alliance)	17,017
Peter Tatchell (Labour)	7698
John O'Grady (Real Bermondsey Labour)	2243
Robert Hughes (Conservative)	1631
James Sneath (National Front)	426
Lord David Edward Sutch (OMRL)	97
Lady Birdwood (Independent Patriot)	69
Michael Keulemans (New Britain)	62
Bill Giddings (Independent Labour)	50
Robert Gordon (Communist)	50
George Hannah (Ecology)	45
Fran Eden (Revolutionary Communist)	38
Ann King (National Labour)	25
Alan Baker (United Democratic)	15
David Wedgwood (Free Trade Anti-Common Market)	15
Esmond Bevan (Independent)	8

No Vote majority	4564

know all about. And as a fool there is one thing I can tell you: you can fool some of the people all of the time, and all of the people some of the time, but you can't fool all of the people all of the time – at least not outside a one-party state.'

DARLINGTON COUNTY

STILL REELING from the implications of my close encounter with Commander Boaks I decided to continue my political comeback by standing at the next by-election, which was being held at Darlington.

I took the morning train with Pauline Healy and arrived at lunchtime to find the press massed on the platform outside the first-class carriages waiting to greet me. I confounded them by stepping out of second-class clutching a plastic cup of tea. I was also deeply honoured at being met by the members of a brass band. It was only when they walked straight past me and got on the train themselves I discovered they were not there to greet me, but leaving town after attending a convention. Fortunately my equilibrium was restored at the barrier by the ticket collector asking for my autograph.

Excitement in Darlington was at fever pitch following the Gang of Four's string of poll-toppers and there were high hopes for the SDP candidate Tony Cook, a typical flash Owenite who was a news presenter on Tyne Tees TV and a wow with the women. Commentators pointed out, however, that he had no political experience or detailed knowledge of his party's programme – although that seemed no great handicap to me as neither apparently did anybody else. So when Shirley Williams breezed in to support him I took

the opportunity of formally handing her a copy of
the Loony manifesto in the hope it would solve the
SDP problem.

'Try this,' I advised. 'Even an idiot can understand
it.'

But Shirley rebuffed me, reaching instead into her
handbag for a closely typed sheet of paper which she
then thrust at me, declaring: 'We do have a platform
– and here it is!'

I read it with a growing sense of unease:

3 pts milk
Hoover bags
Loo rolls
1 large loaf (granary)
1½ doz eggs (no 3)
Woman's Own
one light bulb (25 watts)
6 botts. Concorde British wine

Fortunately for us all, at that point I intervened to
remould the course of British politics. 'Fascinating!' I
breathed, staring at the piece of paper. 'Shirl, this is
marvellous stuff! Here is the meat and drink of politics
on which we all can build!'

'Do you think so?' she replied in a worried fashion.
'Dr Owen doesn't seem to think so. He just keeps
telling me to get myself smartened up and stop being
so scatty.'

'But I think it's wonderful!' I enthused. 'The real
beauty of it is that there's something here for everybody!' Manoeuvring to get her where I wanted, I then
pleaded: 'Shirley, can I keep this so I can study it in
depth? You see, there's so much to take in I must have

some time.' To clinch the deal I added with a winning smile: 'I'm sure you must have another copy.'

'Oh, yes,' she replied, churning round the contents of her handbag. 'There's bound to be one in here somewhere.'

She was still rummaging as I thanked her and nipped off smartly round the corner. The second she was out of sight, I tore the piece of paper into shreds and threw it in the bin – for which you should all be eternally grateful. For that was to prove the one and only time the Alliance came anywhere near understanding what the British public wanted.

Get Back

The front runner at Darlington was the Labour candidate Ossie O'Brien, a former local headmaster. He called an immediate truce with me by saying he welcomed me, 'especially if I could beat the SDP candidate'.

It felt good to be back in the north where I always feel at home despite my London upbringing, which is probably something to do with Mum's side of the family. And with its tradition of clubs I thought it would be a great part of the country to wheel out my new rock'n'politics megaplan. Until then I'd always kept the two strands of my life apart, but after the shock of Bermondsey I knew I had to pull out all the stops. My innovative strategy was therefore to give free rock and roll concerts in pubs instead of boring meetings, and to implement it I sent out an SOS through the local paper for musicians to form a Darlington branch of the Savages for the duration of the campaign.

After being besieged by offers, I kicked off the first rock and roll election gig at my HQ of the Dun Cow, featuring my songs 'Election Fever' and 'Rock the Election', both of which had been released on Atlantic in 1970 and sunk like stones.

In conjunction with the music plan, I now swung my betting strategy into place. The local William Hill's was offering 3 to 1 against my getting more than 200 votes, which to the outsider might have seemed fair enough after my Bermondsey 97. But I already sensed things would be different in Darlington and so I placed £50, which would be enough to win back my £150 deposit.

Video Killed the Radio Star

The main opportunity offered by Darlington was the chance to size up so much of the competition as all the unofficial parties were piling in their big guns. Michael Foot didn't look too good when he turned up with his walking stick, slow on his feet he appeared quite bewildered as he was shepherded into a naff Austin Maestro provided by the local British Leyland Arthur Daleys. Foot wanted to capitalize on a huge row about redundancies at the local railway works at Shildon, one of the few profit-making parts of BR, where five hundred jobs were to go. But the management refused to allow him in, so he held a meeting on wasteland outside the gates during the workers' lunchbreak.

I went to hear his rousing old-fashioned speech before sidling up to him and congratulating him on dropping the duffel coat. 'Well done! I like the whistle and flute!' I mouthed in a stage whisper, but he just stared at me as if he'd never seen me before. I instantly got the message that he didn't want us to be seen together and gave him the sex maniac's handshake to confirm I understood our position. When you are a Loony you soon learn to be discreet.

There was another message for me at Shildon. Pauline Healy had laid her hands on some new information about moves to close some local railway stations, which I tried to bring to the attention of the press. But none of the papers would pick up on it and instead just went on printing Loony stuff. I remembered Boaksy going on about this kind of thing at Bermondsey. He had always been a truly Independent candidate, funding himself out of his own earnings and pension, with no outside support or sponsorship. Independents like us, he had told me, had more right to be heard than the others because we were paying for ourselves. Boaks had been very scathing about empty-headed politicians who just peddled the party line and babbled on about nothing they actually believed in or had thought up for themselves. Yet he, who believed in something passionately, found that TV and radio companies turned off the mikes when he started talking about his concerns, and the papers never reported his statements.

I'd never thought about it before, but now I realized what he said was true. I'd saddled myself with the Loony tag, and the media was determined I would remain in that slot no matter how much sense I made – not that I was planning to make that side of things a full-time occupation.

Make It Easy On Yourself

How to get rid of a politician calling at your house

1. Wave about a copy of the *Sunday Sport* and say: 'Yes, I read a lot about politics'. A scruffy house can also take you a long way, though it won't necessarily save you from a visit from the Labour party candidate. But keeping the windows dirty, the curtains ragged and piles of old beer cans in the front garden may persuade them you're not worth bothering with or can't afford to vote.

2. The 'five yeses' routine. Whatever question you are asked – are you on the electoral roll, will you be supporting their candidate, will other people in the house be supporting them, etc., etc., you just keep answering yes. Eventually they get suspicious they might have got a nutter and slip in a test question like: 'Do you think we should drop the bomb and have lots of lovely fireworks?' to which you excitedly reply: 'Yes! Yes! Goody! Goody!' and clap your hands in an imbecilic fashion. The next thing you should see is a clean pair of heels disappearing down the pathway. Furthermore you get scrubbed off the list as a nutter for all time.

3. Move on to the offensive: a large barking dog is your Number One weapon – preferably a Rottweiler or pit bull terrier. A fear of dogs is one thing politicians and postmen share in common.

4. If you do not possess one of these beasts the following lines are useful:

➤

Come to the door in a soiled vest, preferably with a roll-up fag hanging from the corner of your mouth and grunt, 'Whaddya want?' When they've finished their pitch say, 'Give me a tenner now and I'll vote for you. Otherwise piss off.'

'We don't buy, sell, or discuss politics on the doorstep. Goodbye.'

'Listen, man, I've got toast burning in there. I've not eaten all day.'

Inform them you are part of a police undercover operation. Increase the effect by furtively hissing 'Drugs Squad' and asking if they're carrying any funny cigarettes.

The Green, Green Grass of Home

I got on better with Neil Kinnock, the man destined to be Foot's successor, when I bumped into him in the pub. We bought each other drinks whilst he chatted on about how he was a great fan of Little Richard and Bill Haley and a paid-up member of the Gene Vincent fan club – though I noticed he studiously avoided passing comment on my own records.

Kinnock talked and laughed a lot, but listening to him I could not see him as a raver. If anything he was more a ballad singer – a bit like his fellow Welshman, Tom Jones, but without the balls. The hairstyle was definitely Phil Collins, the style more Engelbert Humperdinck.

As he blathered on my attention wandered and I imagined him in some vile Welsh social club, head thrown back, tonsils quivering and suit buttons popping as he launched into a blood-curdling finale of the 'Last Waltz' and the terrified audience fled for the doors. Perhaps it would be better for everyone, I thought, if he was jammed into a glitter suit and given a gold sax. Then he could vent his talent on blowing in the wind, rather than going on and on as he was doing.

Walk On By

But at least Kinnock was friendly, which was more than I could say for Winston Churchill junior. Young Churchill was never considered a match for his grandfather. And as he was a Tory right-winger, CND was giving him a hard time at Darlington over the emotional issue of Cruise missiles at Greenham Common.

Churchill was followed everywhere by a CND vehicle covered in balloons and with a loud PA system. He eventually managed to lose them in the town centre, only to take a wrong turning and come back for us Loonies to spring out of a shop doorway and ambush him. I suppose his patience had already run out, but the reaction he gave me was still one of the coldest I have ever had from any politician. All I tried to do was give him a cuddle, both to acknowledge him as the grandson of my idol and get a bit of real Churchill rubbing off on me, but he went so white with fury and stared at me with such quivering hate that for once I decided to leave it.

It might just have been the usual thing of my being a litmus test for a politician's sense of humour. Like most right-wingers Churchill conspicuously lacks one, but deep down he may instinctively be aware of my Inheritance from his grandfather. If so it would only be natural for him to be jealous at having been passed over, and of course he has not had a major war to help him.

During the most recent conflict, the Gulf war, I was amused to read in the papers that when he went out to visit our troops he introduced himself to one soldier by saying. 'Hello, I'm Winston Churchill.'

'Oh yes, and I'm Rommel!' the reply promptly came back.

One Two Three, It's So Easy, Baby

I went to the count with my followers after implementing the last element in my new strategy by holding my victory party in the Dun Cow on the night before polling day. The party had been a huge success – especially compared to the SDP meeting which had only attracted four people. A local newspaperman commented there were more people in the toilets at my gig. I'd also had a televised debate with the SDP and Tory candidates and a 'victory' breakfast with the SDP candidate and the broadcaster Peter Sissons, who told Pauline Healy, dressed as she was in fishnet stockings and gloves, she was 'the sexiest woman I've ever met'!

My followers were already in a cheerful mood and they became even happier as the pile of votes in my tray steadily grew. As usual the individual ballot papers were being put into bundles of a hundred, tied together with a rubber band. When I saw I had three of these in the tray I knew I was well ahead and relaxed by going for a wander around. When I came back I saw to my horror that two of my bundles had disappeared. With

When I went to America the glamour and charisma of my normal jetsetting façade wasn't enough for a seriously demented, ill-disguised Loony like me. To really rock the Yanks I took along my Union Jack Roller

My stage act entailed personal, passionate and sensitive performances, as can be seen here as I gently woo an audience in Italy in 1966

The line-up of the Raving Savages changed many times over the years – here I am with my trusty horn section to my left, and Andy Arvard on bass to my right, Jimmy Evans on drums, and a bashful Ritchie Blackmore on guitar

We were performing in 1962 at the Star Club at the same time as the Beatles

The show was the looniest stage act of all time, I like to think – and inspired my slogan 'Vote for the ghoul, he's no fool'

I supplied Jimi Hendrix with his Experience

Muhammad Ali is saying here, 'Please, please don't leave me alone in the same room as this animal!'

The line-up at Wembley in 1972 was the all-time greatest rock and roll bill in this country, and somehow I was on it

The King and I
(and Rodney Bingenheimer)

Drinking with Jagger

Jamming with Page

Strangling with Moon

I entered politics kicking and screaming at the beginning of the '60s

Bill Boaks, a loony from the old school *(Press Association Photos)*

Michael Heseltine, a loony from the new school

As I said to the *Sunday Mirror* after my freedom march on Number 10, 'When you've got talent, who needs a gimmick!' *(Syndication International Ltd)*

Denis Healey, in eyebrow-to-eyebrow talks with the Loony party *(Press Association Photos)*

Alan Hope, the first loony councillor, monsters Geoffrey Howe

Nobody watches party political broadcasts, but wait till this one hits the screen

I've always been lucky with the youth vote – here's another whose vote I'll be counting on one day *(David Hurst)*

only one I would only be marginally better off than at Bermondsey. More importantly, I would lose my bet. Never mind the electoral process, I thought, this is my money on the line.

I went straight to the officials and demanded a recount, which was granted, holding up the result to the despair of the TV producers with their live coverage, whose talking heads then had to keep waffling on about nothing. But I was triumphantly vindicated because in reality a massive 374 Darlingtonians had had the sense to vote Loony. By-election freaks who saw me on the TV in the early hours will have noticed my smile was broader than usual, and it was even broader the next day when I went to Hill's to pick up my winnings. With a little help from my friends I had not only saved my deposit but hoisted up the Loony banner another notch. Winston, I knew, would have been proud of me.

More interestingly, the missing two bundles of votes were found on the Labour pile. Whether this was accidental or deliberate can never be proved, but it did give substance to the warning Boaks had given me. Now, confirmed in my own mind that like him I was on the winning side – albeit unofficially – I knew I must strike whilst the iron was hot. It was time to expand operations by persuading all other good Loonies to join me on the hustings.

Result of Darlington By-Election, 24 March 1983

Oswald O'Brien (Labour)	20,544
Michael Cathel Fallon (Conservative)	18,132
No Vote	13,000
Anthony Peter Cook (SDP-Liberal Alliance)	12,735
Lord David Edward Sutch (OMRL)	374
Arthur Henry Clark (Independent)	164
Thomas Leslie Keen ('Tactical Voting Annihilates Bennite Thatcherites)	27
Jitendra Jul Nim Bardwaj (Yoga & Meditation Party)	15
Peter Reed Smith (Republican)	10
Labour majority	2412

SITTING ON
TOP OF THE WORLD

AT DARLINGTON I had found myself drawn to various other Loonies with whom I struck an obvious chord. The Leeds Tupperware party and the Spike Milligan for Prime Minister party had been floating about, along with the Sleeping party, the Rubber Glove party and the Mad Hatter's Tea party. There were also assorted Loony individuals like Rupert the Hun, who came from Doncaster to canvass for me in an Attila the Hun outfit which included a battleaxe and reminded me fondly of my early Savages days. But even he was overshadowed by Legendary Lonnie, a huge bearded man of six foot six inches who runs a record shop in Stoke-on-Trent and has made a record called Constipation Blues.

Lonnie's Rasputin-like appearance was even more startling as he wore a Wyatt Earp-type coat, and a leather bootlace tie with a big metal cross on it. But his most remarkable feature was a pair of huge saucer eyes which women in particular found hypnotic – they would often run off screaming if he just talked to them. Altogether he was just the sort of weird and wonderful person I was looking for, and Pauline and I now started casting around for more Loonies like him to join in the fun. Not knowing what to expect, we put the word out we were convening a meeting of potential Official Monster

Raving Loony party candidates at Chippenham Mews one afternoon.

To our surprise about thirty people turned up and somehow packed into the front room, along with a crew from Thames TV filming for the 'Six O'Clock Show'. Pauline's cats, horrified at this nightmare of Looniness, legged it and were lost for two days.

I'm the Joker

There and then I set to work to craft this disparate shower into a seamless election machine. So as not to confuse them with boring dogma, I skipped Winston, Bill Haley, Commander Boaks and the whole long story. 'This is a just-for-fun party and bollocks-to-the-rest-of-them party,' I announced. Everyone laughed and that was the end of political theory for the afternoon.

Instead we settled down in the traditional atmosphere of smoke-filled rooms to hugely excited talk and wild predictions of enormous numbers of votes. As I listened I thought of Bermondsey, where at least 500 people had promised to my face they would vote for me, but only 97 actually had. Having learnt the hard way how seldom electoral promises ever materialize I felt a twinge of guilt at sending these brave virgin candidates into the heat of electoral battle. Like all politicians, as soon as they began to believe their own publicity they would be on dangerous ground. But I hardened my heart and silenced my qualms as I dispersed my brave boys to the four corners of the country with a final rallying cry of 'Vote for insanity – you know it makes sense!'

The colourful parade spilled out into the dingy

mews and only the coughing of the pigeons broke the silence, as I gradually wound down from all the excitement. As dusk descended I finally had the chance to meditate upon the afternoon's events. Was this the legacy Winston had etched on my palm so many years ago? Or was it more to do with Commander Boaks, who had not recovered properly from his accident and was now expected never to stand again? Was the secret still locked in 'How To Survive in Politics Without Being Run Over'?

I had been representing the people who didn't vote because they couldn't when I had first stood at Stratford. Was I now metaphorically mounting the Boaks's tricycle – or was I still taking the Winston Challenge? Whose torch was I carrying these days? Who exactly was my political Mentor? And what, precisely, were they trying to tell me? And what about George Orwell, the author of my favourite book *Animal Farm*, who said: 'Whatever is funny is subversive, every joke is ultimately a custard pie'? Where did he come into it? It was all very confusing, especially for a Loony. I made another cup of tea and put on a Chuck Berry LP to soothe my racing mind.

Fools Rush in (Where Angels Fear to Tread)

In the end eleven Loonies got their acts together to stand alongside me in the General Election of 1983 as OMRL candidates. Not everybody who had come to Chippenham Mews that afternoon made it. I was particularly sorry to lose The Executioner, a huge wrestler in a mask who had demonstrated his

Slippin' and A'Slidin'

Whilst out on the trail the most evil trick I have ever come across is used by some extremists for dealing with those terrible people who have three or four election posters in the windows of their house, along with one like an estate agent's sign in the garden.

Having identified the poster and obtained a similar one from the appropriate party committee rooms, the prankster takes it with him to the victim's house in the late evening, not forgetting his box of matches and can of lighter fuel. On arrival at the site, he rolls the poster up into a tube and fills it with dogshit. He then waits outside the house until the upstairs light has been out for about fifteen minutes, squirts the lighter fuel on the package, places it on the doorstep and sets light to it. Next he rings the doorbell and runs for it.

One of the occupants – usually the husband – will come down to investigate and open the door. Seeing the conflagration, he will not stop to think but instinctively start stamping on it to put it out. Timing here is crucial. If the prankster has got it right the poster will have degenerated to a charred consistency and the contents will be warm and squelchy. Ideally they should steam vigorously when released into contact with the open air.

strength by lifting me up in the air as if I was a feather. However, he did volunteer for the important job of being a minder and dealing with hecklers.

I also missed not having Wild Bob Burgos, a '50s drummer whose father, Viterbo, had come to Britain from Argentina and was a Labour councillor in Croydon for eighteen years. Wild Bob has backed stars like Chuck Berry and is known as 'the Tattooed Sledgehammer of Rock and Roll' due to being covered from head to foot in tattoos, even with one inside his lip. Wild Bob had been really keen and was already having his manifesto tattooed on his back, but had to drop out when his band, Matchbox, had a hit single and he went on tour. Nevertheless the eleven of us who did stand made it the greatest concerted show of political Looniness this country has ever seen.

As party leader I was standing in Finchley against Margaret Thatcher – a nasty experience, as Denis can testify. But it was also my duty to go on a nationwide tour which Pauline mapped out to visit all my candidates and do a gig to support them. This worked well except in Bradford, where I had a really bad night. Our candidate, Flying Officer Kite – watch out for the Fokkers behind you! – had teamed me up with a punk band that didn't know any of my songs. When I mentioned Chuck Berry and Little Richard the leader just looked vacant and told me he had never heard of them.

Flummoxed, I did four numbers at 200 mph, with lots of noise and shouting and none of us knowing what we were doing. For me it was my most embarrassing experience in thirty years on the stage, but the crowd still screamed for more, proving to my satisfaction people will listen to any old bollocks. The election speeches and promises by the leaders of the unofficial parties were demonstrating the same point as the election campaign got more and more frenetic.

How Do You Do What You Do to Me?

The high point of my roadshow came at Ashburton in Devon, where the Loony candidate was Alan Hope. Alan was an old friend who had sung support for me under the name of Kerry Rapid at the beginning of my rock career. We had drifted apart until he heard about the formation of the OMRLP and got in touch.

I'd already been down to see him and known we were still kindred souls the second I saw the white plaster bust of Winston Churchill on his desk. 'What's Winnie doing here?' I asked in amazement. Alan just looked at me, smiled, and gave a huge wink. We happily exchanged V for Victory signs and we started chatting about politics, when he revealed he had another link with our glorious political past in that his great-great-great-grandfather had been William Gladstone.

Alan was standing in the Teignbridge constituency, wearing a white suit and a Stetson which led the press to dub him Boss Hogg after the character in the TV series, 'The Dukes of Hazzard'. I preferred his local nickname 'The Great White Hope'.

I arrived in Ashburton to give Alan a hand on the same day that another big name, Geoffrey Howe, was due in town to support the local Tory candidate Patrick Nicholls. (Nicholls later achieved minor fame when he resigned his junior ministership after failing a breathalyser at the Conservative party conference in Brighton in 1990.)

It is not normal OMRLP tactics to go round monstering the opposition, as we like to keep things reasonably clean. But this coincidence seemed too good an opportunity to miss, and Alan and I had cooked up Operation Howe's That? for the occasion. Howe was to remember our cricketing pun and use it later when he finally rebelled against Maggie.

Keep On Running

When our target appeared wearing a grey suit and a silly badge saying 'Howe Now', Alan moved in to shake him by the hand before he started his speech. Howe had then just got going on his speech when I and my followers zoomed round the corner with our battle cry of: 'Vote for insanity! You know it makes sense!'

I had the full Loony gear on and my supporters were even more colourful than usual. There were people dressed as apes and Draculas and a number were what the local paper described as 'scantily clad young women'. It was a real rabble of Loonies, making a terrible din with squeakers, rattles, a fog horn, a huge bell and, as usual, someone playing their own trumpet.

Howe stopped speaking in mid-stream and turned towards us, blinking and looking terribly pained. 'This isn't very professional,' he remarked sorrowfully to me. 'I thought you were an old hand at politics. You should know by now you're supposed to let a chap finish what he's saying.'

I understood what he meant, as he was merely quoting the polite unwritten rules of British electioneering but the truth was it was a mistake, as I simply hadn't realized he was making a speech. However Howe

would not listen to my reasonable explanation and
was so niggled he stormed off. So, with nothing to
lose, we pitched in with Plan B, dogging his every
step on a thirty-minute walkabout. In the end our
victim tried to take refuge in a house before giving up
and re-emerging to scuttle up the road so fast he left
all his supporters behind. After a quick consultation
with his candidate outside the town hall he then cut
his schedule short and fled to Exeter.

'Winston Churchill wouldn't have run away like
this,' Alan and I shouted gleefully after him, but there
was no reply.

Something Tells Me I'm into Something Good

By now fully versed in the fine arts of electioneering, I soon got myself nominated in Finchley and
set up my headquarters in the Railway Tavern, a
music pub just off the North Circular where Tony
Dangerfield, a member of my Savages, was booking
in bands.

I was not the only fringe candidate as Thatcher had
attracted a number of earnest people peddling their
various obsessions. One of them, Colin Hanoman, fell
by the wayside just before nominations closed when
he lost an appeal in the High Court to change his
name to Margaret Thatcher and was lumbered with
a legal bill reported to be £6000. (The same tactic had
succeeded in Glasgow Hillhead where it had been
allowed under Scottish law. The result had been two
Roy Jenkinses on the ballot paper and SDP supporters
being given special permission to stand outside the

polling booths holding signs saying which number on the voting paper was the real Woy.)

The only other candidate left at Finchley who did anything to liven things up was Anthony Whitehead, who stood for Law and Order in Gotham City and zoomed round with a friend in Batman and Robin outfits, promising to save Finchley from Thatcher. But even the Caped Crusader could do nothing to rescue the voters from their streets of echoing dullness. Most of the constituency was dreary suburbia and incredibly straight, and I decided I might have made a strategic error with my new policy of bringing back the village idiot.

To inject a bit of colour I carried round a large tin opener to open up the Iron Lady, which got me a good reception in the rougher pubs. There I found people hated Thatcher and kept asking me to 'give that cow a good pasting'. But most of all they grumbled to me that although they disliked her so much they could never get to meet her to complain to her face.

I decided to test this when the PM made a much-heralded 'public' appearance at a department store. The first confirmation came when our campaign minibus was stopped at a police roadblock and we were told the road was closed as 'standard security procedure'. We humped our props and megaphones on foot and joined the large crowd outside the building. When Thatcher arrived in her Jaguar there were screams for her to resign, but she just ignored the abuse and whisked straight inside. Twelve minutes later she slid out again, posed briefly for pictures, and was gone. I began to see what the people of Finchley meant. 'She gets more like the Queen every day,' someone remarked. 'She'll have her face on the

Houses of the Holy

The Official Monster Raving Loony Party Candidates' Roll of Honour, 1983

CANDIDATE	CONSTITUENCY	VOTES OBTAINED
Screaming Lord Sutch	*Finchley*	235
Flying Officer Kite	*Bradford North*	194
The Masked Man	*Oxford and Abingdon*	267
Tarquin Fintimlinbinwhim Bimlim Bus Stop F'Tang F'Tang Ole Biscuit Barrel	*Cambridge*	286
Dick Vero 'More Dick in Dulwich'	*Dulwich*	99
Alan 'Boss Hogg' Hope	*Teignmouth*	241
Juan Frenulum	*Banbury*	383
Pete the Pub	*Vauxhall*	266
Legendary Lonnie Cook	*Stoke-on-Trent Central*	504
Peter Pooh Perfat	*Kingston*	259
Wally Welly	*Esher*	664
Jeremy Stooks (Official Loony Monster Green Chicken Alliance)	*Poole*	177

stamps next,' another person added to a chorus of assent.

You Ain't Nothin' but a Houndog

I decided to cash in on Thatcher's aloofness by spending a lot of time on the streets. When I'm out campaigning my usual style is to go for people with a bit of a smile on their face. I often make a beeline for those with dogs as they tend to be more friendly and I have never yet had a person set their dog on me. I use 'dogs should have a vote – votes for pets' as a line to make them laugh and that breaks the ice.

My favourite places to work are shopping precincts and street markets, where there is always lots of colour and cheerful banter which I enjoy, as well as the chance to meet all sorts of people. These unfortunately include what are known on the American election circuit as 'panhandlers'. I call them wallies. Election wallies tend to wear grey macs, usually with the belt undone, and are the bane of candidates' lives, as they are normally wandering about killing time and beam in on you as a diversion. In my case these people always make the fatal mistake of taking me seriously and follow me round like an albatross asking stupid earnest question, while all the time I know they are not listening to the answers. I usually throw them off in the end by telling them to come to one of my gigs.

Then there are the wino wallies who stagger up to you reeking horribly of Special Brew or British sherry. I beat these to the punch by saying, 'Have you got a fag, mate, or 20p,' which throws them off balance, as they are supposed to be the ones blagging me. But if

they give me a roll-up – which happens sometimes –
I then give them a pound coin and a badge.

I dislike these wallies particularly as they put the real
punters off. When I'm campaigning I try personally to
meet as many voters as possible and as stopping for
food wastes time I usually snatch my meals on the hoof
– something I capitalized on in Finchley. 'You wouldn't
get Mrs Thatcher campaigning whilst she was eating a
hot dog,' I remarked cheerfully to a middle-aged lady
in a twinset one day as I was sinking my teeth into
my lunch.

But this kind of casual approach doesn't always
pay off. As the lady quailed backwards from the fetid
fumes, by mistake I dropped a slice of onion down
her front and then made things worse by trying to
brush it off with a greasy hand. She looked down
her nose at me as if I was something which had
crawled out from under a stone and informed me
that under no circumstances whatsoever would she
ever vote for me.

'Is that a definite no, or a Loony-maybe?' I asked as
I always do, but with a mighty snort she just swept
me aside and sailed on her way.

I hadn't expected her to vote for me anyhow as
she was a real Thatcher clone, but I did learn one
lesson I am now happy to hand on to other candidates: when you're out on the stump always pass
on the onions – and the red sauce as well if you're
really wise.

Chirpy Chirpy Cheep Cheep

The Tory image makers had by now caught up with my rock'n'politics strategy and arranged a watered-down version through a Conservative Youth Rally at Wembley. This mindless occasion was supported by various pro-Maggie celebs, including Jimmy Tarbuck and Kenny Everett, who woodenheadedly caused a storm by shouting: 'Let's bomb Russia!' and 'Let's kick Michael Foot's stick away!' to loud cheers from the Hooray Henries.

The high point of the event was a song composed and performed by Lynsey de Paul, which went:

> Vote Tory, Tory, Tory
> For election glory.
> We don't want U-turns
> So we'll vote for Maggie T.
>
> Vote Tory, Tory, Tory
> The only party for me.
> Say no to Labour
> And no to the SDP.

This merely confirmed my opinion that de Paul is another dolly bird singer who has only ever got anywhere on her looks. However, her song was not as gruesome as the one composed by the newspaper reporters, who were moaning that Thatcher was ignoring them in favour of the TV cameras.

To try to make their point they sent her a protest song they wrote to the tune of 'Daisy, Daisy':

Maggie, Maggie, give us an interview,
We're all crazy to have a word with you.
We don't need a lot of copy,
But Maggie, we're gonna get stroppy
If you don't, *toute suite*,
Get to your feet,
And give us a par' or two.

Maggie, Maggie, give us an interview,
Your not speaking's making us all feel blue.
You talk to the guys from the telly,
But to us – not on your nelly.
So please relax,
And give the hacks
A minute or two with you.

Maggie, Maggie, speak to us, Maggie do,
We've got questions we'd like to put to you.
We know you think us a menace,
And reptiles – according to Denis,
But really we're sweet,
So why don't we meet,
Just give us an interview!

Thatcher of course continued to ignore them in spite of this bizarre musical mixture of threats and grovelling.

I Did It My Way

At the count in Finchley the Thatcher exclusion zone was maintained when the announcement of the result was stage-managed in the council chamber at Hendon

General Election Result at Finchley, 9 June 1983

Margaret Hilda Thatcher (Conservative)	19,616
No Vote	17,207
Laurence Spigel (Labour)	10,302
Margaret Joachim (SDP-Liberal Alliance)	7763
Simone Wilkinson (Women-Life on Earth and Ecology Party)	279
Lord David Edward Sutch (OMRLP)	235
Anthony Joseph Noonan (Ban Every Licensing Law Society)	75
Helen Mary Anscomb (Independent: Rail not Motorway)	42
Anthony Peter Whitehead (Law and Order in Gotham City)	37
David Alec Webb (Anti-Censorship, Reform of the Obscene Publications Act)	28
Brian Clifford Wareham (Party of Association with Licensees)	27
Benjamin Collingham Wedmore (Belgrano Bloodhunger)	13
Conservative majority	2409

Town Hall. All of us other candidates jammed together in small boxes whilst she had a large one to herself – a separation I had never known before. Maybe, I thought, she was frightened a bit of Loony dust might rub off on her and give her a sense of humour.

However, I did manage to corner her backstage before the results and say, 'Glad to meet you at last, Mrs Thatcher.' Smiling vaguely she touched the cuff of my leopardskin jacket and remarked it certainly was made out of bright material. 'You should put some of your ministers in outfits like this,' I suggested. Thatcher replied with a dry chuckle that that would certainly brighten up the House, but I could see that, like Queen Victoria, she was really not amused and was not relishing being seen talking to me. Denis was much more friendly and called me David.

Fortunately it is my prerogative to be as obnoxious as I wish on occasions like this and I was determined not to be beaten. So when she was leaving after her victory speech I positioned myself halfway down the stairs and then pushed forward to congratulate her, forcing her to shake my hand and making sure it was all being recorded by the TV cameras. As I did so I thought how ironic it was that I had to go to the trouble of standing as a candidate simply to do something the voters of Finchley apparently could not – actually meet their MP in person.

Paperback Writer

There was one particular journalist at the count who seemed to be let into everywhere, which I couldn't understand until I was told she was Mrs Thatcher's daughter Carol, who was writing a book on the campaign. When the book was published I heard it had a photograph of me in it, but the gushing copy about 'Mum' and pages of girlie rubbish about hairstyles put me off, so I didn't buy it at the time.

Years later I was cruising through Soho when I saw great piles of this tome in the window of a dirty bookshop – one of those ones with a beaded curtain over the entrance where men always look both ways before diving in. Doing the same, I entered and accepted the bargain offer of twelve copies for a fiver, which so mystified the owner I felt obliged to explain. When I showed him my picture in the book he asked me to sign one of the many copies he had left. As I handed it back with a flourish to this seedy little porn merchant, I suddenly thought – that's where books like these are going to end up one day, down with all the dregs in seedy little shops like this.

But immediately after the election the comment in the *Mirror* on the OMRLP's electoral success was more to the point: 'Many people will say that Mr Sutch and his friends ought not to be allowed to make mock of the electoral system. But they have a right to stand and the people have a right not to vote for them. Except for lunatics, of course, who don't have a vote. Does Mr Sutch realize that?'

Did I realize it indeed! The *Mirror* had hit the nail on the head. As I was to explain to the first OMRLP annual conference, thanks to Winnie, Bill Haley, Commander Boaks and all the leading politicians I had now mingled with, I also realized a whole lot more.

Twenty Things You Didn't Know About the 1983 General Election

1 According to opinion polls compiled by Gallup, only 54 per cent of the electorate thought there were important differences between Conservative and Labour.

2 Less than 20 per cent of the electorate approved of Michael Foot, the Labour leader, an all-time low.

3 Parliament was dissolved on Friday 13 May.

4 There were 475 candidates not attached to one of the three main parties or the Scottish or Welsh Nationalists.

5 The Ecologists with 108 candidates, the National Front with 60, and the British National Party with 53, qualified for an election broadcast by fielding more than 50 candidates.

6 For the first time the three main parties fought every seat in England and Wales.

7 Two former party leaders, Sir Harold Wilson and Jo Grimond, retired and did not stand for re-election.

8 Mrs Thatcher had fewer front-page pictures than in 1979, despite carefully chosen photo-opportunities which included a farm in Cornwall, a bakery in Newcastle, and an electronics factory in Reading.

9 Richard Attenborough, who had just received a clutch of awards for his film *Gandhi*, announced the Mahatma would have voted Alliance if he had been around.

10 After the polls had closed at 10.00 p.m. the first declared result was Torbay at 11.15 p.m., followed by Cheltenham and Guildford. All were held by the Tories.

→

11 A total of 209 Labour MPs were elected, 49 less than in any election since World War II. Labour's share of the vote was 27.6 per cent, less than any election since 1918, and less per candidate than in any election ever.

12 The Conservative share of the vote, 43.5 per cent, was almost the lowest for any party winning a clear majority, but still got them 397 seats – the largest number held by any party since the war.

13 A total of 150 new MPs, 23 per cent of the House, were elected from a total of 2577 candidates.

14 The youngest new MP was 24-year-old Charles Kennedy, SDP MP for Ross, Cromarty and Skye, and the oldest 56-year-old Peter Hubbard-Miles, Conservative MP for Bridgend.

15 Of the Conservative MPs elected 70 per cent had been to public school.

16 The number of old Etonian Labour MPs doubled – from one to two.

17 The election cost the government £2.3 million for returning officers' fees, plus an annual cost of £24.3 million for the electoral registers.

18 The government received £110,850 from lost deposits.

19 The highest turnout was Fermanagh and South Tyrone (88.6 per cent), the lowest City of London and Westminster South (51.8 per cent).

20 The closest result was Leicester South, where the Conservatives had a majority of seven.

HALFWAY TO PARADISE

HARD ON the heels of our General Election success the Tories called a snap by-election at Penrith, where old Willie Whitelaw had been pensioned off to the Lords the second he'd been re-elected. It was a typical cheap trick, but I was ready for it – at my peak and raring to go with all nutters on standby.

Pauline and I jumped on to the Scottish express and headed north from Euston, arriving in town with only two hours to collect our ten signatures before nominations closed. But there are times when you know God, as well as Winston, is on your side. As we rushed out of the town hall a crowd emerged from the pub opposite asking for my autograph. I swopped their signatures for mine and within a few minutes had all my nominations without even moving off the municipal steps.

The voters of Penrith were happy to see me as they were fed up with having to go through it all again and welcomed me as their saviour from yet more boring old farts. Many told me they thought that that 'silly old bugger' Whitelaw should have been retired years before, but when they informed me that they felt they had been conned by the Tory media machine I had to remind them there was nothing new about that. As I have always said, the sign on election programmes which reads CON GAIN means precisely what it says.

In Penrith the result of this dissatisfaction amongst the local sheep-shaggers was to boost the Loony vote from zero to 412 – an unprecedented increase – which gave further confirmation to suspicions that I was leading the fastest growing party in the country. Some quick calculations on the back of an envelope revealed that if our expansion continued at the same rate I would be Prime Minister by the year 2010. I made another visit to William Hill.

Behind the Green Door

There was another spin-off from the election with the creation of the Green party. I had already had Sutchy and Sutchy advise Mrs Thatcher green was not her colour as it made her look washed out. She had since followed their recommendation by steering well clear of environmental matters.

Sutchy and Sutchy had also informed me that the name of the Ecology party, which had put up 108 candidates, was hopeless. I agreed, having met few people who understood it, many who couldn't pronounce it, and even more who couldn't remember it. Anyhow, I have always steered well clear of anything ending in '-ology' on principle, as I have found that it always means they are coming to get you one way or another.

What was needed for the Ecologists was a more simple word, Sutchy and Sutchy explained, and we had the answer in our election candidate, Jeremy Stooks of the Official Monster Raving Green Chicken Alliance – I must say Jeremy had put on a clucking good show. Jeremy had been the first candidate to ever use 'Green' in his party title, so we now offered his platform to the Ecology party to solve its brand-name recognition problem which Sutchy and Sutchy had identified.

Obviously we couldn't let the Ecologists use our own brand names of Official, Monster, and Raving, and we were already in dispute with Dr Owen about the use of 'Alliance'. But we could offer the rest, and the Ecologists accepted. Being vegetarians, they then dropped 'Chicken', thereby forming the Green party. After having met some of their candidates, however, I think it would have been more honest to leave the 'Chicken' in. And experience has shown me that although they may appear to be a bit alternative, in many ways the Greens are just as bad as any other party.

At one by-election I offered a manifesto to a road-sweeper, whereupon he nearly hit me and furiously pointed to the street, which was knee-deep in election bumf like confetti. He wouldn't mind a badge, he said, but a leaflet was the last thing he needed. 'They're a real menace,' he complained. 'People just glance at the shitty things and then throw them away, leaving me to clean them all up.'

I picked up one of the leaflets littering the ground and saw it was from the Green party. Then I saw they all were. They might have been printed on recycled paper, but that hadn't stopped piles of them being thrown into the gutter just like any other old rubbish.

Benny and the Jets

The by-election at Chesterfield, held just as the miners' strike was starting in March 1984, was the high point of political Looniness in the '80s. As the Official party I knew there was great jealousy amongst the unofficial parties at our success and behind the scenes the system began to rally itself to try and crush us. Symbolically I stood as Monster Raving Loony Last Stand party.

Labour joined in the Loony spirit of the occasion by nominating my old enemy Tony Benn, the man who had killed off pirate radio stations and like me was another veteran of the hustings. Benn had lost his Bristol seat in the General Election nine months previously and was now standing for the fourteenth time.

Benn was Number One Unofficial Loony, at least according to the *Sun*, but I must say that over the years I have become very tired of the 'Loony Left' tag being attached to people like him and Ken Livingstone without my consent. It has been a shameful stealing of our name, raising the ghastly spectre that unofficial politicians would seize the Holy Grail of Looniness which is rightfully ours. Furthermore, whenever I met any of these so-called 'Loonies' I never understood what all the fuss was about, as every single one of them always seemed so straight.

I had a good time playing a gig at Ken Livingstone's final party for the GLC making his newts jump around a bit, and I found him pleasant enough. At Chesterfield when I went to one of Benn's meetings he was far from the green-eyed monster he was made out to be. Rather, he reminded me of a maths or geography schoolteacher.

The only thing we seemed to have in common was that we were both prolific tea-drinkers and lived in Kensington – although like Michael Foot as a true socialist he has a house which is considerably larger and more valuable than mine. Benn told me a long and involved story about how his loony image in the media was all a capitalist vendetta directed at him personally, but it was all so complicated I didn't understand a word of it. Anyhow I was miffed that he obviously did not trust me, as he ostentatiously tape-recorded the whole conversation on the grounds that I might misquote him afterwards. True Loonies are never as paranoid as that – we *know* that everyone really is out to get us.

Old Shep

Once Benn had thrown down the Loony gauntlet a record number of Loonies rushed to join in the fun. I saw what was coming when my old mate Sid Shaw came on the blower. Sid runs the Elvisly Yours warehouse in Hackney, where he has a huge gold statue of Elvis in the foyer and floor-to-ceiling racks of mags, records and 'collectable items'. It's where you go for those things you've always wanted like knickers inscribed 'I love Elvis' and 'Love me Tender'.

'I'm thinking of putting Elvis up for this by-election,' he told me.

'But Sid, surely he's dead, isn't he?' I replied.

'What difference does that make?' he asked, puzzled. 'So are half the MPs in the House of Commons.' Being a great optimist, he was then struck by a fresh thought. 'Anyhow,' he added brightly, 'Chesterfield's so far north the news about Elvis may not have got there yet!'

Sid's campaign was based on his analysis that as there were millions and millions of Elvis fans he was bound to get millions of votes and would therefore save his deposit. It was the old trap for first-time candidates, but he was not to be deterred, so we did a deal to split expenses and went for a Laurel and Hardy double act. Sid dressed in a marvellous shiny baseball jacket which was a replica of Elvis Presley's last touring jacket, although to be honest it still didn't stop him looking like a young Benny Hill with his glasses and all.

When we were campaigning if people said they wouldn't vote for me I told them to vote for Sid instead. 'Elvis is making a comeback,' I'd explain. 'He's only got six feet to go.'

But the trouble we all had was that there were so many politicos on the streets it was virtually impossible to meet anyone who was not a candidate, canvasser, agent or journalist and with all the other Loonies about I sensed I had a real fight on my hands. Most of the competition held its meetings in boring halls so in addition to my rock'n'politics gigs I upstaged them all by holding the world's first political meeting in a chippie.

As the chips were down, I declared, we would batter our enemies into submission. I then held up a fish, inviting the voters to 'Plaice your bet on me'. Seeing the gratifyingly huge press coverage the next day, I knew we had hooked them in and scaled fresh heights.

The In Crowd

The most curious of the other fringe candidates was the actor Bill Maynard, who played Selwyn Froggett in the TV comedy series 'Last of the Summer Wine'.

Maynard was standing as Alternative Labour candidate and taking the whole thing very seriously, sincerely believing he would get at least 2000 votes. He bet £1000 on the back of this belief and although he got over 1000 votes he was extremely upset not to do better, and told me afterwards he would never stand again.

Other members of the weird and wonderful crew included Giancarlo Picarro, a 21-year-old student at Worcester College of Education, who was standing as Official Acne party, having suffered terribly from a tender age. After spotting him all over town I gave him a special honorary Blackhead Award. David Cahill, the Reclassify the Sun Newspaper as a Comic candidate, claimed the paper was so incredibly biased it should declare its interest. There was also Christopher Hill of the Prisoner: I am Not a Number party who had become confused by Patrick McGoohan's cult TV series 'The Prisoner'.

Some Loonies appeared directly opposed to each other's interests. Helen Anscomb (Death off Roads: Freight on Rail party) seemed in danger of being run over by David Bently, a 37-year-old car salesman representing the Four-Wheel-Drive Hatchback Road Safety party. I had a momentary touch of sadness that Commander Boaks had now retired from politics. A run-in between Bently's Japanese Shogun-style vehicle and Boaksy's armoured tricycle would have been an epic.

By far the silliest candidate of all was standing on the ticket of a Chesterfield for Chesterfield and put a leather sofa on the back of a pick-up to go campaigning. But this was a useful bonus for us as we could sit on it, thereby both depriving it of publicity and having a comfortable ride at the same time.

Winchester Cathedral

From my base at the White Swan – inevitably dubbed the Mucky Duck – I ran a brisk campaign with only one major blunder, which just went to show that no matter how Loony you are, you have to be very careful what you say in an election in case people take you at your word. Asked in a TV interview what I would do for Chesterfield, without thinking I replied: 'If you elect me, I'll straighten that crooked spire of yours.'

What I had forgotten is that the spire is the only thing the place is famous for and in a supermarket the next day I was attacked by a flotilla of grannies, one of whom bashed me with her handbag and knocked my topper off. 'You leave our steeple alone – we love it as it is!' they shouted at me.

Sid and I then upped the ante by hijacking an Alliance meeting being addressed by the Liberal leader David Steel, using the loud hailer to ask a series of embarrassing questions from the floor. It was all just for fun, and Steel took it in good heart, telling me afterwards he admired our cheek. I was so impressed by his attitude that I later invited him to a Monster Raving Loony fund-raising evening at the Hippodrome, where he throughly enjoyed himself and we made him an honorary member of the party.

Before the real vote all of us fringe candidates held a mock election in a local night club, with a DJ as the returning officer, in which Sid and myself were declared joint winners. We agreed to share our seat in the Commons and I told the press hacks we would alternate by my sitting on Sid's knee one day, whilst he sat on mine the next.

But the inevitable result of the real election was victory to Benn, although as the result was announced a voice echoed from the back of the hall: 'The wrong Loony's won!' Everybody cracked up as the cameras zoomed in on me. 'Thank you for the compliment,' I said politely.

I did notice, however, that Benn did not seem to share the joke, which I thought a bit poor as the Loonies standing in the by-election were no madder than some of the oddballs and single-issue campaigners he had courted inside the Labour party. Amongst a rabble of feminists, lesbians, gays, militant vegetarians, bicycle-riders and assorted peace campaigners, his supporters even included the Posadists, who believe socialism will be brought to earth with the help of aliens from outer space. Even us Loonies have our feet more on the ground than that!

The House of the Rising Sun

After Chesterfield I knew the party desperately needed a proper forum for the discussion of our policies and so I decided we should follow the example of the unofficial parties by holding an annual conference. I briefly considered their regular venues of the three Bs of Brighton, Bournemouth, and Blackpool before choosing Ashburton. This put us in the lead alpha-betically and we also found the town perfect for our new World International Global (WIG) headquarters which would be a beacon for our many supporters.

Although I'm a Londoner born and bred, I've always liked the south-west of Britain as it's so laid back and therefore has good Loony karma. Ashburton is not

Result of the Chesterfield By-Election, 1 March 1984

T. Benn (Labour)	24,633
M. Payne (Liberal Alliance)	18,369
No Vote	15,828
N. Bourne (Conservative)	8028
B. Maynard (Independent)	1355
L. Sutch (OMRL Last Stand)	178
D. Bently (Four-Wheel-Drive Hatchback Road Safety)	116
J. Davey (No Increase in Dental Charges)	83
T. Layton (Spare the Earth-Ecology)	46
H. Anscomb (Death off Roads: Freight on Rails)	34
J. Nim (Yoga and Meditation)	33
D. Butler (Buy Your Chesterfields in Thame)	24
P. Nicholas-Jones (Independent – The Welshman)	22
S. Shaw (Elvisly Yours Elvis Presley)	20
C. Hill (Prisoner: I am Not a Number)	17
G. Picarro (Official Acne Candidate)	15
D. Cahill (Reclassify the Sun Newspaper as a Comic)	12
J. Connell (Peace)	7
Labour majority	6264

only a pleasant market town but also contains the veritable rock on which the OMRLP is founded – the Golden Lion, owned by the man who became our chairman at this time, Alan Hope. It was at the bar of the Golden Lion, where staunch British folk had been getting pissed for over 300 years, that the Loonies found their true home.

Examining the other conferences we found them composed of interminable formal sessions, think-tanks, speeches, group discussions, workshops, and fringe meetings. We banned the latter on the grounds we already were the fringe, and junked the rest on principle. Instead we settled on a three-day conference in which official business was restricted to one session of no more than two hours. This gave the press a chance to get back to the bar and for us to prepare for the more important informal evening sessions when Alan and I got up on stage to belt out the everlasting virtues of rock and roll. The session always ended with the 'Voting Raving Loony Song', sung to the tune of 'She'll Be Coming Round the Mountain':

> We'll be voting Raving Loony when it comes . . .
> (*first verse*) We'll be getting rid of Thatcher/
>   Major/etc when it comes . . .
> (*second verse*) We'll be sitting in Number 10
>   when it comes . . .
> (*third verse*) I'll be your new Prime Minister
>   when it comes . . .
> (*fourth verse*) We'll be reducing all the taxes
>   when it comes . . .

Imagine

Unlike other politicians I have never sought world domination, but many people came to the conferences very excited about this possibility. The Wally in the Middle party, for example, made an important point. The country was obviously stuffed with Wallies – you only had to walk into any branch of Dixons, or count bobble hats and fluffy dice in Ford Capris to see that. If every Wally voted for us power would be ours!

Yet, as they were Wallies, how could we get through to them? What did Wallies stand for? They certainly didn't stand for the National Anthem, but then who did these days? The debates went on far into the night. I had my own strong views on this. I find Wallies, in general, hard to define, but I can spot them a mile off, and like everyone else I have met my share. My particular pet hate comes from my frequently having to make phone calls from awkward places all over the country.

The Wallies are the pinheads who have spent a fortune on buying long, unfunny celebrity cassettes for their answering machines, or have half a record by their favourite band as the message. The result is my having to wait for ages, as well as spending 50p, just to ask them to ring back. I am still waiting for the invention of the device that tells you there is an answering machine at the other end and gives you a chance to ring off before your money is lost.

But things like this are minor annoyances compared to the real damage a Wally can cause as they never seem to know where to draw the line. Once after a show I was in my dressing room with all the gear on when I was approached by a family who asked if they could be photographed with me. I obliged by posing with mother, father, and daughter when I noticed a midget standing just outside in the corridor. I could sense he also wanted to say hello and have a photo but was too shy, so I said to him: 'How're you doing, mate? Fancy a photograph?'

He replied he didn't mind, but I knew he was really keen. As I towered over him and he was very conscious of his height, I sat down and got him to stand beside me while I asked the photographer to take a head and shoulders shot.

I had just put my arms round the midget to make a warm picture when some Wally came round from the back of the stage shouting: 'That's right, Dave – pick the little squirt up and put him on your lap!'

I've never been so embarrassed in all my life, especially when the Wally repeated it in a great bellowing voice and then guffawed with laughter at his own joke, The midget and I went bright red with embarrassment, but the worst thing of all was the Wally was a member of my band.

No, I insisted to the other Loonies, we did not want Wallies at any price. Mind you, they still keep turning up from time to time, but then they do everywhere.

Ticket to Ride

The conferences also led to my interrogations by the reporters from the big papers being stepped up. These middle-class hacks were always asking what the hidden meaning of it all was and insisting that us Loonies were an important factor in the electoral process. Their difficulty was in defining exactly what that was. This always brought us on to the meaning of politics which, like the meaning of life, can be debated for ever. Fortunately the party as such was not overburdened with members wanting to delve into the minutiae of political theory. Most of them happily adopted the correct attitude by thinking the Marx Brothers invented communism and 'Yes, Minister' was a documentary series.

So how precisely did you define a Loony? the big paper reporters kept asking. After fruitless attempts to explain that it was all relative, in the end I would illustrate our nature by a true story. Throughout my career I have often relied on British Rail to carry me the length and breadth of the country. Unlike people such as Margaret Thatcher, I enjoy train travel and the chance it gives me to meet all kinds of people. And it is the railway company I have to thank for what everyone experiences – a seemingly trifling incident which marks a sea change in their lives. For me that incident was a Crewe change.

I was trying to sort out the Loony thing in my mind one night as I was returning from a gig in the north and had to change trains at the famous railway junction. It was close to 3 a.m. as I humped my heavy bags up the footbridge steps to be confronted by two grown men huddled on the parapet. They were heavily wrapped up against the bitter cold and had been there so long I could see the hoar frost adhering to their moustaches. As I struggled past with my load neither lifted a finger to help, but I saw one of them stare at me and then turn to his friend and remark: 'Look – there's that Loony bloke who's always standing for Parliament'.

I was just about to say something when I heard the rumble of a train approaching. Instantly both men forgot me as they turned away to lean over the bridge and get the number of the engine. Then, taking up their biros in their gloved hands and blowing on the ends of them to make them work, they wrote down the number in their train-spotting notebooks with great mutual excitement.

I continued across the bridge, ensconced myself in my new warm compartment and, as the train drew out, looked up and saw them both still standing there in the freezing cold. If I'm the Loony, I thought to myself, then what the hell are they?

The big paper reporters would nod respectfully at this, but still not give up the relentless questioning. So what did the Loony party represent? they would demand. We were the party of protest, I would explain, Officially representing the Unofficial side of the non-voters, who often won the count at real elections. More sage nods would follow, along with more questions: what did I hope to achieve? what did we stand for? what was I in it for?

Finally I would deliver my hammerblow. ' "Politicians can only take money because people picture their corruption as being altogether finer and nobler than it really is" ', I would tell them, quoting Bertolt Brecht's *Threepenny Opera*. At that point they would nod even more sagely than ever before quietly giving up and going away.

They're Coming to Take Me Away, Ha! Ha!

There was something else I had now grasped which was more historically significant. The key to political success lay in organization, as the Tory party had brilliantly illustrated. Its sole reason for existence was to gain power and hang on to it at all costs, so it was the best-organized of them all. But it was here I parted company with the Tories and all the other unofficial parties. For a start, like many musicians, I do not function well – if at all – before midday. So if I took power, all important world events would have to take place after lunch, preferably in the late evening. (As it happens, I am excellently equipped for the hours kept by the House of Commons.)

In addition there is my own sense of timing, which has been known to try the patience of even my best friends. I have never been a clock-watcher and I keep what I describe as a flexible attitude to appointments. That way, by not having set up the expectation of being on time, I do not disappoint when I am late. (Things would of course be different if the country adopted the Loony policy of decimal time, which as well as being easier to cope with, would add extra days to the week.)

Added to this should be my inbuilt ability to get lost in what should be familiar places, and – the final political masterstroke – my being a plastic-bag person. I am a great plastic-bag fan, hanging them on my walls as a useful substitute for pictures. I have even held an exhibition of my international collection at the Candid

Warehouse gallery in Islington, run by my Minister of Arts, Marie and Duncan. You will seldom see me out and about without at least one plastic bag containing my current business, a system which I find works perfectly in my personal and professional life. But even I will admit it does have severe limitations if you are engaged in setting up an organization capable of taking over the country.

In the end it is these various practical factors which have, at least for myself and the OMRLP, solved the whole knotty problem reporters from the big papers endlessly agonize about. By their very nature Loonies are not organized, as otherwise they would obviously rule the world. But at the same time organization is self-defeating, as it only increases the risk of both I and the party taking ourselves seriously. That in turn would lead to us no longer being qualified to be Loonies, and therefore ruling ourselves out of the equation.

The Winner Takes It All

But despite all this grand talk I knew my fellow Loonies still needed a bottom line to console them during those black moments when they temporarily lost sight of the higher purpose. We all had to know there was a way we could seize power if we ever chose to lower ourselves to it – though of course I assured members we never would. Fortunately Alan came up with the answer from the archives of the Golden Lion. The surefire way of seizing power, he told me, was a return to pre-Victorian values. I was immediately interested. Maggie was preaching a return to Victorian values and so if we went back further in time we would seize the historical high ground.

In the past, Alan explained, Ashburton had been one of the great rotten boroughs and the Golden Lion used to entertain the voters before elections. This simple tactic of bribery had never failed. Solemnly he reached under the bar and produced a copy of the bill for entertainment at the election in 1796.

As there were only 155 freeholders in the constituency entitled to vote this was a truly staggering amount.

'Christ!' I said, genuinely awe-struck. 'There's no way we can afford anything like that with the number of voters these days!'

'You're right,' Alan agreed, running his eye along his line of optics. 'The cellar's not even big enough, never mind the cost. But at least we do have some idea of what the bill would be if we decided to really go for it and resort to traditional democracy.'

Bill for an election dinner in Ashburton, November 1796

	£	5s	5d
Entertainment of Sundry Voters the day before election and morning of election	18	5	58
Dinner	36	10	50
Beer, Porter, Cyder and Pop	4	5	50
Wine			
612 bottles red Port at 3/6d	107	2	50
14 bottles Sherry at 4/-d	2	16	50
12 bottles Madeira at 6/-d	3	12	50
2 bottles Claret at 6/-d		12	50
Spirits			
12 bottles of Brandy at 6/-d	3	12	50
7 bottles of Rum at 6/-d	2	2	50
15 bottles of Gin at 6/-d	4	10	50
Fruit	1	10	50
Sugar	1	15	50
Tea and Coffee	4	0	50
Cards		10	56
Supper, Porter and Cyder, Pipes and Tobacco		10	56

Stores shut up at half-past 6 o'clock after which the following liquor was consumed:

	£	5s	5d
Grog and Punch	3	512	56
55 bottles Port Wine	9	511	56
Negus	2	512	50
3 bottles of Brandy		18	50
Hay and Corn	1	515	50
Total	219	51	52

WILD THING

OVER THE years I have kept away from regular politicians as much as possible outside by-elections as they are an obnoxious group of people and not the sort you would want in your house. Inevitably, though, the ones who have fallen by the wayside have come crying to me as a habitual loser. Shattered and traumatized by what has happened, they are desperately in need of solace and comfort and beg pitifully for my help. I therefore invariably show them the door. But I have relented once – with Michael Heseltine after the Westland helicopter affair in 1986.

I followed this political row with more than my usual interest as I was playing the company's social club in Yeovil at the time. The workers' worries had been increased by Heseltine's clash with Maggie which had culminated in his storming out of the Cabinet to resign, and there was considerable doom and gloom about the shenanigans going on over their heads.

I suggested to the social secretary that in the circumstances he ought to become a Loony candidate, but when he replied he could get his marching orders if he stirred it up too much I confined myself to a few cracks on stage and thought no more about the matter. That was until I had a phone call summoning me to Thenford House, Heseltine's huge mansion in Northamptonshire.

Distant Drums

I was curious to meet this most nakedly ambitious of British politicians, so for once I accepted. I took the train, to be met at the station by his man and transported to the house in a Range Rover whilst I appreciated the lordly view from the high passenger seat.

As the appointment was semi-political I was in full Loony gear, and I saw Heseltine wince as an aged retainer ushered me into his vast study. Just for good measure I greeted him with the sex maniac's handshake.

Heseltine poured himself a large Scotch, and I accepted the offer of a cup of tea, specifying Assam. After dismissing the retainer he got straight down to the point. 'My opinion polls amongst my servants always tell me that apart from that old bag Maggie you're the best-known politician in the country,' he informed me, motioning me to sit down in a leather armchair by the roaring open fire.

As he carefully hitched up his moleskins to sit opposite me, I noticed the retainer hovering near the door and making feeble inquiries as to whether I required biscuits. Heseltine promptly picked up a log from the grate and hurled it at him. After the door had hurriedly closed and he was certain we were alone, he leant forward and gave me a chilling stare with his piercing eyes.

'Your secret, man!' he demanded. 'Tell me your secret!'

I looked at him, thinking how different he was to my guide Commander Boaks, who had died a few months earlier having never really recovered from his road accident. It had been a sad event, but I did admire the way the nature of his demise personally proved his belief that roads were dangerous. If his pedestrian crossing proposal had been in effect he might still be with us today. Instead the Commander had been a man who had died for his beliefs – something I couldn't see Heseltine doing, no matter how much some people would have liked him to disappear one way or another.

As the retainer staggered back in with my Assam – but not, I noted, any biscuits – I ran my eye over the golden-locked wonderboy of the Tory party, examining what he'd already nicked from my act. He'd done the hair gimmick to perfection and copied my mike-swinging by whirling the Mace round in the Commons and becoming famous as Tarzan. So what else could I do for him?

'Maybe you should take a leaf out of Ronnie Reagan's book and ham it up a bit more,' I suggested cautiously. 'You like dressing the part – remember that butch flakjacket when you were smashing up CND back in '83? Why not go the whole hog and get into Lurex leopardskin like this?'

I held out my sleeve for him to have a feel, but he just shuddered and fastidiously picked a golden hair off the front of his handknit fisherman's Guernsey. Then he impatiently downed his whisky and jumped to his feet, glaring up at the chandelier as if expecting Heavenly guidance.

'I know you're a Loony, but there's no need to be a cretin as well!' he shouted at me. 'Now jump to it with something sensible, man, or I'll have you mucking out the stable where I keep the stalking horse.'

I had heard about this mythical beast, which was later to be brought out for a run in the Maggie stakes, but having no wish to meet it at that point I decided I had better give Heseltine a straight talking to.

Hey Man, Take a Walk on the Wild Side!

'Well, Michael,' I told him bluntly, 'with your background – Eton, Oxford and all that – you've never met anyone except other rich prats like yourself. I, on the other hand, have been out there gigging amongst the people for thirty years. So if you want to be in my position, why not give that a go?'

There was a squeak of leather as Heseltine collapsed dazed into his armchair. 'You're not suggesting I go into places like pubs and clubs and rub shoulders with the Great Unwashed?' he demanded incredulously.

Seeing how pale he was, I rushed to reassure him. 'No, Mike baby, not the plebs as such – just the hard core Tory faithful. You've made your pile, you don't have to do any work, so you're free, man – free to get a show on the road and let your fans see where you're at.'

'Tell me more,' Heseltine replied, sitting down and readjusting his moleskins. Suddenly there was a nasty gleam in his eye and I knew I'd captured his interest.

Michael, Row the Boat Ashore

'Go gigging, man,' I advised him. 'Get the Heselteenies together and play the Tory clubs. Look at Tony Blackburn or Jimmy Savile. They're just like you. They can't

162

sing, dance or even tell jokes. What they can do, though, is slap on a record and give out loads of bullshit. You can do that and – I can say without taking the Michael – you have got more charisma than all of them put together. So get out there, throw your hair about, then jam to all your favourites like "Jumping Jack Flash" and "Satisfaction". Add a few flashing lights and the odd strobe, lay on plenty of verbals over the mike, Mike, and you'll be a star as quick as you can say Jimmy Young!'

Heseltine plunged his head into his hands and let out a mighty groan. 'No, no, you bloody Loony,' he cried. 'I'm canning all that wild Tarzan stuff. What I need now is to get people to trust me.'

At that point I realized he did indeed have a serious problem. 'Cool it then,' I suggested instead. 'Just talk to them and push your line – decent person, honourable resignation, don't want to stab Maggie in the back . . . They'll love it, Mikey baby.' I gave him a conspiratorial leer. 'Natch, you'll need to wow the Blue Rinse brigade, so don't forget to give the fatties a quick cuddle and a nice wet smacker to show you care.'

Heseltine dashed his hand impatiently through his mane. 'Conservative clubs are full of ghastly people these days,' he replied sharply. 'Workmen, nasty little businessmen, tradespeople, shopkeepers – it'd be like a permanent election campaign.' With a shudder he added: 'You'll be saying I should kiss babies next!'

I took a reflective sip on the Assam. 'Look, Mike, if it gets too heavy you can always do a runner. Go out the back, swing the old liana over the wall and you can be gone in the Range Rover without even getting your green wellies wet.'

Heseltine paused for what seemed like hours, staring

into the leaping flames with his gimlet eyes. Then he suddenly leapt to his feet. 'Wow! Now I've thought about it I really dig that, baby,' he shouted. 'You've put me in the groove, man!' Rushing to the fireplace he picked up the poker and I ducked as he started whirling it round his head. 'Hey, man, that's where it's at,' he cried triumphantly. 'I can see it now! The Heseltine Rubberneck Roadshow! It'll be a sell-out everywhere!'

The Mighty Quinn

When he had calmed down I gave him the rest of the gen. 'Knock off a quick book to tell the punters how brilliant you are. It doesn't matter if it's crap – just sling in loads of pictures. Then flog off autographed copies to give the fatties something to take to bed at night. That'll make you the last thing on their minds as they go under. The books'll pay for the roadie and the petrol, so the whole shooting match costs you zilch. And if you want to move into profit you can soon bang out a few T-shirts and badges.'

'Dave, now I see why everybody thinks you're so fab!' Heseltine replied with a gratified smile, throwing the poker back into the grate and pressing the bell for the retainer. I drained the last dregs of the Assam and rose to leave.

As I was obsequiously ushered out into the magnificent hall, he hissed conspiratorially: 'Don't breathe a word about this meeting or I'll have your goolies. The last thing I need is the punters thinking I'm a flash lightweight cavorting with a Loony, eh?' He broke into convulsive laughter as he confidently took up position astride the broad steps of the mansion, his magnificent mane billowing in the wind. 'See you on the road, Dave,' he shouted as I clambered into the Range Rover and set off down the drive.

As we rolled past the sculptured hedges and manicured lawns I heard a strange noise behind us: 'Oo-eeu-oo! Oo-eeu-oo! Oo-eeu-oo!' For a second I was baffled until I realized that for the first time I was hearing a Tarzan call rendered with an old Etonian accent.

I sent Heseltine a modest bill from Sutchy and Sutchy for services rendered but when I never received a reply I put it down to experience, vowing never again to do business with a Tory.

We Can Work It Out

My advice to Heseltine was based on the fact that, as I had thought it would, my horror spoof had crossed all time barriers. Never in or out of vogue, I had successfully kept it going over all the years whilst dozens of other fads, ranging from Chubby Checker and the Peppermint Twist to the Bay City Rollers, had all proved to be two-minute wonders.

But round the time of Westland in 1986 things had looked up for me thanks to the '60s revival which put lots of old bands back on the road – the Searchers, Gerry and the Pacemakers, the Swinging Blue Jeans, the Fortunes (whose agent had once been Reg Calvert), the Tremoloes, the Merseybeats, Dave Berry and the Cruisers, Marty Wilde . . . the hunt was on for any old rocker who could be dragged out and dusted off for the latest craze.

The rules about band revivals were pretty rough and ready, but there was an unwritten agreement that to qualify for its old name a band had to have at least one of its original line-up. Some were therefore 'revived' with one wizened old figure playing alongside a group of fresh-faced youths, while others had somehow survived intact and had more or less the original personnel. Some, of course, were completely beyond it – either dead, or sunk into the pits like the legendary P. J. Proby, who I've seen so out of it he had to crawl on stage on all fours.

My agent Barry Collins how put together a Monster Roadshow for a series of mini-tours of town and city halls. The package was based on a group of us who were real old raves from the grave, including Johnny Walker of the Walker Brothers, Ricky Valance and Don Lang ('Tell Laura I Love Her'), Tommy Bruce ('Ain't Misbehavin' and 'Chantilly Lace'), Christian St Peters ('I'm the Pied Piper'), Wee Willie Harris who did a cult record called 'Rocking at the Two I's', Jet Harris, formerly of the Shadows, whose biggest hit was probably 'Apache', Cliff Bennett ('Got to Get You Out of My Life'), the Vernon Girls ('Short Shorts' and 'Itsy Bitsy Teeny Weeny Yellow Polka Dot Bikini') and Jess Conrad, who had gone on to play Joseph in *Joseph and His Amazing Technicolour Dreamcoat* and star in a number of films, as well as running the famous Showbiz Eleven football team. These were also echoes of the recordings of the late Joe Meek in myself, Heinz the lead singer of the Tornados and Mike Berry (with his hit single 'Tribute to Buddy Holly'), as all of us had had records produced by him.

Time Is On My Side

Most of the people who turned up for the Roadshow gigs were in their forties or even fifty, and they loved it. They often dragged their kids along, who looked totally bored until we blasted them with the visuals, which is where my part was especially important.

But I found it all very mild compared with the old days. I'd slimmed down my act so I could carry round all my props in a suitcase, but the coffin routine had been replaced by coughing half the time. Like the rest of them I found I simply could no longer do what I'd done when I was twenty-five. In those days I'd load the van with my big PA and all my props, go round and pick the band up from their houses and drive all the way to somewhere like Blackpool on the crappy roads before motorways. When I got there I'd unload, set up the gear, do two 45-minute spots, and chat up a bird before reloading and driving all the way back to London, usually arriving back at first light. These days just the thought of driving to somewhere like Blackpool tires me out.

But it was not simply that I and the audience had got a lot older. With all the safety regulations that had crept in over the years and the fuss about decibel levels most of my original act was no longer allowed. For all the government's excited talk about the new world of freedom, rock and rolls shows were enormously tame compared with the past.

But I was also using rock constructively to deal with that other problem of getting older: putting on weight. Finding myself getting a bit tubby round the middle I had gone to sign on at a gym in Harrow in desperation.

The place was full of lumps of lard huffing and puffing as they tried to turn themselves into reasonable shape, along with those body-building posers who make me feel ill every time I look at them. I was not at all keen and when I was told a course cost £200 I became even less interested. Then I suddenly thought how stupid it would be to go there to pick up lumps of iron or run on rubber fanbelts when I could simply sweat it off on stage as all that leaping about does more for you than any Jane Fonda workout. So I phoned my agent, fixed up a few more cheapie pub gigs, and was able to have fun, lose weight, and make a bit of cash all at the same time.

The Best Things in Life Are Free

The extra money was also very useful, as we Loonies suddenly needed a lot more of it. The idea of getting rid of people like us from the political scene by increasing the election deposit had been around since before the 1983 election. After much debate in Parliament the deposit had finally been raised from £150 to £500 in October 1985. It could have been worse as the Commons Select Committee had proposed raising it to £1000. And it had been pointed out that as the original £150 deposit had been introduced in 1918, if it had been linked to inflation it would now be £2000 – which gives you some idea of how successive governments have safeguarded the value of your money.

The electoral system has changed its rules many times, and not just to include new voters and candidates by widening the franchise. In the early '60s, as I was entering politics, servicemen found out they could get a free discharge by standing for Parliament, and losing the £150 deposit was cheaper than the alternative of buying themselves out. Nine servicemen stood in all, scoring a total of 1426 votes at an average of 158 each, before the loophole was hurriedly closed. But even then the deposit had not been increased.

The stated purpose of the deposit was to deter frivolous candidates, but who qualified as frivolous was hard to determine. We Official Loonies could – and did – claim we were making a serious point. Many of the other fringe candidates spending their own money were intensely serious – possibly none more so than Amanda Fielding, who stood from time to time on the platform of Trepanning on the National Health. Trepanning is a medical operation involving boring a hole in a person's skull, and the candidate, having had it done herself, believed in it passionately and with an intensity perhaps only made possible by her heightened consciousness.

Increasingly the deposit is a dangerous precedent in any system, as it puts the squeeze on those with the least resources. Naturally in Britain the party most in favour was the Tories, but both the Alliance and Labour objected to it being raised to a level which would cripple them. As the Official party we are not the only established one to lose deposits regularly. Dr David Owen's Gang of Four SDP-Alliance was used to forfeiting them hand over fist, and even Labour had lost 119 deposits in 1983 at a cost of £17,850.

I formed the Monster Raving Loony Fighting Tooth and Nail Fund to get across the message that the increase was a vindictive and undemocratic attempt to cripple us as the leading Loonies. But it was in vain, and we were forced to look for more money.

Can't Buy Me Love, Oh!

Of all the questions I am asked, the most frequent, both about myself and other Loony candidates, is: 'Where does the money come from?'

The answer to that is simple: out of our own pockets.

We Loonies are proud to be part of a long tradition of eccentricity stretching back into British history. I have always put this down to the British class system producing numbers of well-heeled people with nothing else to do. Loonies may not be well-heeled, but we accept that our activity has never been properly subsidized and we have to be self-supporting. Candidates therefore tend to be people running their own shows, usually in the music or entertainment business.

I suppose it is because people are so used to politicians being crooks and lining their own pockets that I find many people won't accept that the mystery of our funding is so simple. To be fair, we have never been hounded by the press, accusing us of having our pockets a-jingle with Moscow gold, being a CIA front, or even a splinter group from MI5. But there still seems to be a suspicion lingering in many people's minds that we must be some sort of conspiracy and our funding must come from some devious source.

If only that were so! The Loony party has 8000 paid-up members paying an annual fee of £3, or who have opted for bargain life membership at £10, but the only slush fund we have ever known has been the stuff that seeps into your shoes after a heavy snow-fall. Big business has consistently ignored us, obviously realizing we do not intend to give it all the tax breaks

Like a Rolling Stone

Official Monster Raving Loony Object of the Decade

THE SINCLAIR C5

The only notable exception to our 'no business-men' policy was Sir Clive Sinclair, who hugely excited Loonies everywhere with his boffin-like appearance and madcap projects. I never actually asked Sir Clive to become a member of the party, but having briefly adopted the Conservative idea of think-tanks, I did sit down with him at one stage to work out what we could give the people.

I had intended to bring Commander Boaks into our wide-ranging discussions, but unfortunately he was still *hors de combat*, otherwise the exercise might never have led as it did to the creation of the Sinclair C5. This innovative and patently absurd vehicle had the correct Loony design constituents of being brilliant in concept and design, whilst totally lacking in common sense and practical application.

For me it still remains a glimpse into the future. I have no doubt that one day it will be back, especially as it attracted even less purchasers than I get votes.

like the Tories. In the end we actually lose, as Loonies in general tend to be major supporters of various brewing conglomerates. The difference between ours and the Tories' business links is that we pay them, rather than the other way round.

TEARS OF A CLOWN

THROUGHOUT THE mid '80s I continued my core activity of pounding the streets at by-elections, all the time building up to the test I knew would be coming at the next General Election, which Maggie was bound to call once Nigel Lawson had organized the credit boom to fool the punters into thinking they were winning something.

At the by-election in the Vale of Glamorgan – which is really Cardiff – I recruited Shakin' Stevens's old band the Sunsets to back me whilst Dave Goddard, the bass player, doubled up as my election agent. My promise to the electors to build the other six bridges to complement the Severn was rewarded with 266 votes. At Brecon and Radnor, way out in the Welsh wilds, I campaigned for votes for the sheep which far outnumbered the local electorate and as it was such a rural constituency I used a horse and cart to go touting for votes.

But whilst this went well, just before the election the OMRLP was plunged into the dilemma all of us had been dreading. Having agreed our candidates were fighting on the basis of being outside the system, we knew there would be trouble if one of them won. Under strict Loony logic they would then have to leave the party, as they would have become part of the system. Matters came to a head when our chairman Alan Hope became the first of our candidates to fail conclusively by being elected to Ashburton Town Council in the local elections in May 1987. The party was immediately thrown into crisis. Under Loony principles Alan must now be ejected, which would be a disaster. Not only would I lose a faithful friend and colleague, but the party would be left without both chairman and its WIG HQ of the Golden Lion.

Fortunately we found a solution through the irregular method by which Alan had been elected. There had been twelve vacancies on the council, but only twelve candidates, who had all been returned unopposed, making Ashburton the first Loony-Conservative controlled council on party lines (the other ten were Independents). Alan therefore argued successfully before our Ethics Committee that, as nobody had actually voted for him, Loony rules had not been breached. He had been elected by default, which was not his fault.

After a long session at the bar, during which out of the warmth of his heart Alan generously provided free drinks for the committee, it was agreed he could both remain in the party and take up his new office. Using his newly gained political insight, he then announced that the General Election would be held in October, and we launched our manifesto on the spot to throw our enemies off the scent.

As we got stuck into the matter of composing our policies at the bar, I idly voiced the opinion that the unofficial parties' manifestos were a tissue of lies. Dick Vero, our 'More Dick in Dulwich' candidate, then put forward the novel ploy of producing the world's first honest political manifesto. This would be seen as truly Loony, he pointed out. Furthermore, in view of Alan's close encounter with failure, the best way to make sure our candidates weren't elected would be to have a manifesto which scared the shit out of people.

It Ain't What You Say, It's the Way That You Say It

It was a tempting idea, but not silly enough for me. I had anyhow decided from the beginning the party would not major on either policies or manifestos. As all the other parties simply made promises they had no intention of keeping, I saw the Loony role as throwing some fresh thinking into what was otherwise a sterile debate.

I had therefore adopted a free and easy attitude inside the party to both policies and the holding of Shadow Offices of State. The OMRLP allows anybody joining to appoint themselves to whatever Shadow Office they wish and put forward whatever policies they want. The leadership simply supplies core policies for manifestos on which candidates can expand and add local issues.

Some people just want something simple like a heavy metal club or a swimming pool in their town, whilst others have completely batty ideas, like Potty Bill who wanted a disused factory razed to the ground to make a landing strip for UFOs. He earnestly explained to me that he often saw them hovering hopefully just after the pubs had closed, but they always missed his town and went somewhere else because there was nowhere to set down.

For the '87 election we proposed turning Britain into the world's biggest tax haven by driving the Channel Tunnel through to the Channel Islands (although an alternative faction argued we should carry on to Switzerland and establish a direct underground link with all that gold stashed in the bank vaults).

We also expressed the hope Britain would go non-nuclear, since we had found that Mrs Thatcher kept the nuclear button next to the alarm clock on Denis's side of the bed. Instead we proposed limiting weapons to flour bombs and water pistols, which we agreed would be much less dangerous.

Whilst we were at it we also moved to scotch a scurrilous rumour that we were changing the name of the Loony party to 'Don't Know' to get more support. This sort of attack is always tiring, as we have to keep pointing out the obvious fact we must be seriously Loony, otherwise we would have changed our name to something like the Sensible Person's party or the Common Sense party long ago.

Don't Let the Sun Go Catch You Crying

In theory we should have swept the board in the General Election. Sutchy and Sutchy had come up with a new slogan of: 'Don't be stupid, be a smarty; come and join the Loony party' and in press interviews Alan was predicting a massive swing to lunacy and promising: 'Today Ashburton – tomorrow the world' – or at least Plymouth.

But although we were putting a brave face on things in public, behind the scenes I knew we were in deep trouble. Every great movement has its setbacks, and I had to face the fact we Official Loonies had been decimated by the vicious deposit campaign. The raising of the deposit to £500 was therefore a

She's My Best Friend

What the Conservatives' 'honest manifesto' would have promised for the decade ahead had they used it in the 1979 General Election:

* Inflation rising to 21.8 per cent within a year of election
* Unemployment rising to over 3 million, worse than during the Great Depression
* War with Argentina at the cost of 560 British lives
* The collapse of British industry, handing over British Leyland to the Japanese and selling Jaguar to the Americans
* Introducing American Cruise missiles on to British soil
* Selling off the nation's assets at give-away prices
* Reducing tax rates for very rich bastards and cutting assistance and benefits for everybody else
* Record bankruptcies, company liquidations and mortgage repossessions
* Destroying the National Health Service
* Bringing in the Poll Tax and massive new rates to crucify small businesses (then changing our minds and scrapping it at fantastic cost)
* Destroying traditional state education, causing thousands of teachers to flood out of the profession
* Creating 25-mile-long traffic jams on the motorways, never mind the M25 itself
* Making a hole in the ozone layer and threatening the end of the world through global warming
* Putting the country into recession through high interest rates, messing up going into Europe, and deposing the Prime Minister without consulting the electorate

Nobody but a Loony, we concluded, would have voted for that.

crippling blow to many of the finest in the land and although many people outside the OMRLP agreed it was shameful discrimination, there was nothing we could do as superb potential candidates dropped off like flies.

We were not the only people affected. The Puss in Boots party, which was planning to win by a whisker, never made it. We lost Happy Ron, the owner of a novelty shop in Bournemouth who sold me all my skulls. Another candidate we were very sorry about was Rory Blackwell, a former member of the group Lord Rockingham's XI, which had a number one hit with 'Hoots Mon! (There's a Moose Loose Aboot this Hoose)'.

Rory had been prospective Loony candidate for Torbay, where his main policy had been to move Thatcher Island, which lies just off the resort, to the mainland. He was just the sort of man we had been looking for as he already held world records for playing 24 musical instruments at one time and 318 instruments one after another as part of a single tune, and was preparing to go for new world records for upside-down drumming (held at the time by Buddy Rich with ten seconds) and marching ten miles playing three instruments at once.

People like him would have enlivened what was otherwise a dull election in which the only real bit of excitement was when Denis Healey nearly got involved in a fight on Breakfast TV. I always liked Healey and at one stage considered copying his eyebrows gimmick to give myself more gravitas until my doctor advised against it.

But I had to hand it to the *Sun* for keeping the Loony banner flying through holding a 'psychic' poll in which

a medium 'interviewed' great figures from the past
to discern their voting preferences. Henry VIII and
Boadicea revealed themselves to be Tory, Labour's
only supporter was Stalin, and Keir Hardie threw in
his lot with Dr Owen and the SDP. I was, however,
surprised to find Genghis Khan was a 'don't know' as
I had always thought him to be a typical Tory.

I Got Stung

To compound the gloom round the bar at OMRLP
World International Group Headquarters I had a personal setback in Finchley, where I had been planning
to star in *Thatcher 2*. With my normal sense of timing
I reached the registration office with fifteen minutes
to spare before nominations closed. But my papers
were then found to have the signature of a voter who,
though on the register, was not yet eighteen. It was too
late to get anybody else so I was disbarred and forced
to watch from the sidelines.

In many ways I was relieved not to have to trail
the dreary suburban streets again and meet Mum and
Carol – though nobody apparently had asked Thatcher
junior for a follow-up book. And I had dreaded the
thought of going through the Maggie security-mania,
which had got worse during the intervening years.
Sadly for all of us I seemed to be the only party
leader left who could actually go and meet the people
without being surrounded by a mass of gun-toting
Special Branch, personal bodyguards and uniformed
police – never mind the massed ranks of hacks and
camera crews shoving everybody out of the way. The
'walkabout' had, in my view, become a 'camera-about',

Twenty Things You Didn't Know About the 1987 General Election

1 The Stock Market rose 50 points when the election was announced.

2 Mrs Thatcher went on stage at major rallies to the tune of 'Jerusalem' or music specially composed by Andrew Lloyd Webber, complete with laser show.

3 There were 54 nationwide surveys on voting intentions, compared to 49 in 1983.

4 Between the announcement and polling day, 200 hours of TV programmes were entirely or substantially devoted to the election. The result was a 20 per cent rise in video rentals.

5 The Labour party election broadcast was written by Colin Welland, directed by Hugh Hudson (*Chariots of Fire*), and had music by Michael Kamer, who wrote the score for the film *Mona Lisa*, which starred Bob Hoskins.

6 The increased deposit led to 2325 candidates, compared with 2577 in 1983.

7 A total of 144 new MPs were elected, with a post-war record of 88 retiring.

8 A record number of 41 women MPs were elected from a record 243 women candidates, along with the first four black and Asian MPs.

9 The oldest MP re-elected was Michael Foot, aged 74; the youngest was Matthew Taylor, Liberal MP for Truro, aged 24.

10 Sir Bernard Braine (Conservative) became the Father of the House, having served continuously as an MP since 1950. He took precedence over Edward Heath, also elected in 1950, as he had been the first to take the oath.

→

11   Of the elected MPs, 132 Labour and 199 Conservative had no parliamentary experience of any Prime Minister except Margaret Thatcher.

12   Of the 130 trade union-sponsored Labour MPs two-thirds had no experience of manual work.

13   Humphrey Berkeley (Southend East) completed a party hat trick by standing for the SDP, after previously being both a Conservative MP and a Labour candidate.

14   In England Taunton had the highest number of the new postal votes with 2687, and Newham North-West the lowest with 231. In Northern Ireland the highest was Fermanagh and South Tyrone with 6715.

15   Party spending increased by 65 per cent – allowing for inflation – from £7.6 million in 1983 to £15 million. Permitted expenses rose from £4200 to £5400 in an average urban borough, and in country seats from £4700 to £5800.

16   The government received £145,000 as a result of lost deposits. Hardest hit was the Green party, which contributed £66,500.

17   The Conservatives won 57 per cent of the seats with 43 per cent of the votes.

18   The highest turnout was Brecon and Radnor with 84.4 per cent; the lowest Hackney South and Shoreditch with 55.4 per cent.

19   The closest results were Brecon and Radnor, which the Liberals won by 56 votes, and Mansfield, won by Labour with precisely the same majority.

20   Torbay was again the first to declare, beating its 1983 time by 14 minutes to come in at 11.01 p.m. It was followed in order by Guildford, Basildon, and Cheltenham.

aimed solely at TV and with no thought of meeting actual people, who were relegated to a sideshow.

But there are always turn-ups in the world of Looniness and a surprise candidate appeared in Finchley in the form of Lord Buckethead, the representative of the Gremloids party. Buckethead arrived at the town hall to hand in his nomination papers in a hired Daimler and seemed an interesting chap, though I did not feel him to be my equal. But we did have something in common in both being Lords, and he enterprisingly adopted Loony dress by wearing a billowing cloak and a bucket-shaped hat which rested on his shoulders and obscured his face. I heard afterwards that because of this some voters thought he was me in a new rig-out, which might explain why he got a reasonable 131 votes.

The result of the election didn't surprise me. I knew Maggie would sweep home again despite the re-theming of the Labour party, which had now adopted its trendy red rose motif and copied my rock'n'politics strategy with Red Wedge and Billy Bragg. But I was pleased to see the old Ecologists, who Sutchy and Sutchy had helped to put on the right road as the Greens, had forged ahead as a result and fielded 137 candidates – albeit at a frightful cost in new £500 lost deposits.

And there was another happy result with the one party I've always felt we could do without – the National Front – withdrawing. The official reason was a terminal split in its ranks the year before, but I thought it was because most members had by now sussed that they might as well join the Tory party or just not bother, as everyday British life had been reorganized to make street riots commonplace without using the pretence of political activity.

Mess of Blues

When checking out the performance of your favourite fringe candidate assess them against the number of spoilt papers, which in the 1987 General Election averaged as follows, per constituency:

England	52
Wales	60
Scotland	35
Northern Ireland	285
Average (throughout the UK)	57

Bits and Pieces

As Official Loonies we fielded five candidates, principally in the West Country. At Cambourne and Redruth in Cornwall Freddy Zapp, a fire-eating DJ known as the Light Fantastic, kept up good monstering traditions by campaigning in a hearse whilst dressed in an undertaker's outfit. Freddy's target was the dead vote, which unfortunately is not as large here as it is in Ireland, otherwise he would have won easily. As it was he got 373 votes.

In Hastings and Rye we had a splendid new candidate in Loony Lord Tiverton, a retired businessman and millionaire, who had graced our conferences with his fashionable cream Rolls-Royce Corniche. 'Tivers', a perfect gentleman of the old school, was particularly interested in importing the sport of dwarf-throwing from America, where it is popular with couch potatoes and even some dwarfs, who enjoy being hurled through the air. His policy did not endear him to all shorter voters, but he still scored a respectable 241.

In Honiton Stuart Hughes, a John Cleese victim and the proprietor of the Fawlty Towers Guest House in Sidmouth – which he was later to paint in the colours of the Union Jack – ran a storming campaign and got a remarkable 747 votes. Stuart attributed much of his success to wearing an elephant's head in his appeal for a 'Jumbo' vote.

Alan Hope, playing a dangerous political game by also having become an official member of the Dartmoor Wally Club, contested Teignbridge again. Alan backed himself to win at odds of 10,000–1 and although he didn't quite make it he did boost his vote from 241 to 312 – a healthy increase of 25 per cent.

In South Hams, Devon, our candidate was Tim Langsford, the landlord of the Queen's Arms in Dartington, who was also a paid-up member of Totnes Conservative Club; Tim advocated turning the entire country into a fun park creating eight million jobs. Ex-politicians would be employed as waiters so people could shout and throw bread rolls at them, and the constituency renamed as South Hams, Egg and Chips. Tim scored 277 votes.

But for me the greatest satisfaction of all was in seeing our old enemy, the Gang of Four, decimated to the Gang of One. Woy Jenkins*, Roy Rodgers and Shirley Williams all got the boot, leaving only the sinister Dr 'Death' Owen out of the original line-up.

---

*I heard later that Jenkins was joining me in the memoirs game with his book *Wank and File*.

Now Owen's sidekicks had been cleared out of the way, he and I could move to a straight one-to-one fight for the hearts and minds of the GBP – the Great British Public. Few people believed me at that stage, but I already knew who the smart money would be fancying.

Other Loony Candidates in the 1987 Election

PLACE	PARTY	VOTES
Exeter	Let's Have Another Party party	209
Windsor	Blancmange Throwing party	328
Tatton	Feudal party	263
Norwood	Rainbow Alliance	171
Islington	Human party	56
Havant	Creek Road Fresh Bread party	373
Harwich	Official Fidgeyitous party	161
Hampstead	Captain Rainbow's Universal party	137
Galloway	The Retired party	230
Finchley	Gremloids party	131
	Gold party	59
Dartford	Fancy Dress party	491
Cirencester	Male OAP party	283
Bedfordshire	Only Official Best party	435

A FOOL SUCH AS I

NATURALLY THERE was great rejoicing amongst the unofficial parties about the reduction in the number of Loonies. But the one thing which really annoyed me was that people still thought standing for Parliament was easy. All you had to do was put down £500, the pub bores were always jawing. Anybody could do it. These people had never met an electoral jobsworth.

The bureaucrats who run our town halls tend to be these sorts of people, just trying to toe the line. Although I have found some pleasant and friendly, and the odd one even showing some glimmerings of intelligence, by and large, and especially when you're standing as a Loony, you're just as likely to meet a jobsworth in full cry.

The new candidate, going to the town hall and receiving his nomination papers from the jobsworth, needs a proposer, seconder and the signatures of eight voters for his name to be put on the ballot paper. He takes the form, gets ten people to sign it and brings it back. The jobsworth then gets out a large book and starts checking the signatures. When you ask what he's doing he replies: 'I'm checking the electoral roll. Your signatories – the people who signed your form – have to be on the electoral roll. You didn't ask for one before, did you?'

'No,' you reply, at which point he hands you one and

you set off again, this time to find ten people who will not only sign but are also on the roll.

This is not as easy as it sounds. Having stopped a person, you then have to hold them there whilst you leaf through this enormous book of names and addresses. All sorts of confusion then breaks out. They start looking over your shoulder and saying: 'Yes, that's my name, Mr Thompson, and that's my road, Parkview Road. Fuck me, who's this? Mr Murphy? That's not me, there must be some mistake. Oh, I see what's happened – you've got the right road, but the wrong area. That's not my district, you see. I must be somewhere else in the book . . .'

You start looking through again, but when you've eventually found his name he's usually got bored and cleared off.

You finally go back to the jobsworth after a day and a half with maybe four signatures and explain you can't understand the roll and lots of people can't find themselves.

'You need the street index to go with the electoral roll,' the jobsworth replies.

'So why didn't you give me one when I got the roll?'

'Did you ask for one?'

'No, I didn't know such a thing existed.'

'Well, you do now,' the jobsworth replies with huge satisfaction.

At last, fully armed with nomination papers, electoral roll and street index, you start again – only to come across a new problem. When you walk towards people carrying these massive books they often do a runner as they think you're going to sell them an encyclopaedia. Since the Poll Tax people are now afraid that you are checking for non-payers.

You swear you're not selling anything but it still cuts no ice. 'We're not signing any papers, we've been caught with HP before,' they tell you firmly. I had one who even changed his mind, grabbed the form back and crossed his name out, as he had suddenly become convinced that having signed a government form he was now on the shortlist for the army, which he believed was always looking for Loonies and trouble-makers.

Come Outside

Sometimes the jobsworths, who close at 2.30 p.m., run out of electoral rolls and simply suggest you come back the next day. Once when this happened to me I asked: 'So what can I do until then?'

'Why not do your checking with the electoral roll kept at the reference library?' the jobsworth replied.

'You're not seriously suggesting I hold people in the street whilst I go to the library to check them out?' I replied incredulously. 'You must be joking!' At this the jobsworth got very stuffy.

'It's not up to me to help you fill in your nomination papers,' he said.

To shortcut his suggestion I went to the library and started asking people there who were reading the papers. They asked all the normal questions, like was I a communist, whilst I ran through the normal spiel in reply: 'It won't cost you anything. They won't throw you in prison. You won't get your name in the papers . . .'

The woman running the library then came across. 'You're not allowed to discuss politics in here,' she said. 'It leads to arguments.'

'I'm not discussing it,' I replied. 'I'm doing it.'

'That's not allowed either,' she replied firmly. 'I've seen you in the street giving out these leaflets. It'd be better if you left.'

I had no choice, but I did get one signature as a result of this bum's rush. A bloke followed me out and insisted on signing because he hated the woman in the library so much. Much to my surprise he also turned out to be on the register.

Anyhow, having finally got your ten signatures and had them all approved by the jobsworth, you then hand over your cheque for £500.

'We don't take cheques.'

'I know for a fact you do from the major parties.'

'We only take a banker's draft or cash.'

'Credit cards?'

'No.'

Inevitably, if you aren't prepared, you end up queuing at the cashtill.

Another Brick in the Wall

It's not all the jobsworths' fault, of course. Your problems are compounded by the suspicious nature of the GBP, half of whom seem convinced you're from 'Candid Camera' or 'Beadle's About', whilst the others treat you as if you've got the Black Death.

'No, I can't have my name associated with it. You're that guy on TV. I've seen you on TV. I don't want to be called a Raving Loony. I don't want them knocking on my door . . .'

My worst time was at Bermondsey, where I foolishly entered the concrete jungle to try a tower block of council flats whilst dressed in my full Loony gear. 'Hallowe'en, is it, squire?' the inhabitants would inquire from behind their security chains.

'No. It's a new party.'

'Looks like it. What is it, then?'

'It's a political party – the Official Monster Raving Loony Party.'

'Oh no, we're not joining anything.' Slam.

'Politics, eh? Not tonight, thank you.' Crunch.

'Fuck off, you batty bastard or I'll fill you in.' Bang.

'Go away or I'll call the police.' Crash.

In the entire massive block I didn't get one signature.

I then tried using the Loony gear to draw exhibitionists in the street. This tactic worked brilliantly as they were attracted like bees to a honey pot. One guy always grabbed the form and then handed it round all his mates. I'd get it back in a flash with maybe twenty signatures on it, but find only five of them checked out on the electoral roll.

But that's not the worst thing that can happen. I had one person who changed his mind after somebody told him he would get kicked out of the Labour party for signing and promptly tore the form up. Or you spend a whole day getting it correct, right down to numbers eight or nine, only for some half-drunk to rush up and sign before you've had a chance to check them out. And if they're not on the electoral roll that ruins it. You have to rip the whole form up and start all over again.

My Way.

Eventually everybody evolves a method which suits their style of campaigning. Commander Boaks, for example, had explained to me at Bermondsey how he worked a system with old people's homes. When a by-election was announced he would go to the library and look up the addresses of geriatric homes in the local telephone directory. He would then write to them politely explaining he would be calling to gather his signatures. This system worked so well, he told me, that not only did he invariably get the signatures with minimum effort, but often afternoon tea thrown in as well. In return the aged residents were treated to a talk on road safety, a subject close to many of their ageing hearts, and both sides parted company mutually satisfied.

I had tried copying this for the next by-election at Darlington, but the result had been disastrous. The old folks, seeing me emerge from the bushes and dart across the lawn, freaked out and I found myself being beaten off by hordes of wild-eyed octagenarians. I had hastily backed off, thinking I was just too wild and scary for these people. But Pauline Healy said the real trouble was my top hat, which made me look like an undertaker touting for business.

By trial and error I found the best way for me was to base myself in either cafés or pubs, where people weren't rushing past and I could sit at a table and take my time to get it right. I also thought it fair on the voters, as it gave them plenty of opportunity to size me up and ask me any questions they liked.

Help Me Make It Through the Night

Despite all the problems, there are plenty of con-
solations in political life and, just as in the music
business, one of them is groupies. And if you don't
think political groupies exist, ask Cecil Parkinson!

Naturally I've known plenty of pop groupies –
though not as many as the majority of bass players,
who are usually the ones in a band who get the
most action. Bass players are often very good-looking
and have the easiest instrument to play. The average
punter never notices if they're all over the place or
just pissed out of their heads, which enables them to
spend their time both posing and eyeing up the birds.
Lead singers like me, who should be the main focus for
the girls, are handicapped by having to concentrate on
singing, which often involves pulling awful faces; the
lead guitarist is usually too busy playing; and the poor
old drummer is just a head bobbing away at the back
and always worst off.

Pop groupies were a rough and ready lot and,
in the more carefree days before AIDS, this led to
regular visits to the gonorrhoea clinic for some painful
treatment, including the male equivalent of a scrape.

Political groupies are not only cleaner but more
sophisticated than pop groupies – which you can tell
because they don't curse and swear when it slips out.
They are also much thinner on the ground, despite
the myth of the gushing redhead in a flimsy daycoat
telling you she wants to support your party, but you
must come in as she can't do it on the doorstep.

In reality most political groupies are slim, secretarial
types, often quite mousey-looking and with glasses

– the sort of girls you see in banks and building societies. But you can take it from me they're usually a much hotter property between the sheets than the blondes in skintight leather micro-skirts who hang round the pop scene where they are known as 'all tits and bum'. Political groupies usually operate by coming to meetings, where they pepper you with questions about policies and what it all means before suggesting you end up at their flat to discuss it further. This in turn tends to be much neater and tidier than that of your average pop groupie, and often has proper books on the shelves – which in some cases they have actually read.

But there are exceptions to this rule, which once gave one of my supporters one of his worst moments, as well as underlining the perils of the most dangerous thing of all in any election situation – the car sticker.

Stuck On You

If anyone gives you a car sticker you should ask for an accident premium. If an election turns nasty you'll be lucky to get away with having your aerial bent and both wing mirrors ripped off, with the extra options of dents all over the body, the whole thing being smeared with dogshit, and sugar or sand being put in the petrol tank. The most straightforward vandalism is a simple brick through the window, which I've seen several times with the National Front and the Bash the Rich people if the car is sporting a Tory sticker. But in my experience it's the Tory louts who are much more likely to go down the side of a Labour vehicle with their car keys.

If you want any of this to happen to your vehicle the most dangerous place to park is outside party committee rooms and particularly the town hall when the count is being held and where there is quite likely to be a screaming mob tooled up with placards on pieces of wood. Whatever the result of the vote you can lose both ways. If their guy wins they can get very excited and shove a placard through your window, but the danger is even greater if their side has lost. Then they're liable to take it out on the nearest vehicle proclaiming itself for the winner – especially if their candidate has only been defeated by a handful of votes and they've been waiting for hours for the result in rain, frost or snow.

The very least you can expect is to have your tyres let down – which is no joke at 2 a.m. in the middle of a strange town.

Satisfaction

But there are other dangers attached to having a car sticker which are not so obvious and which I once experienced in a northern seat which shall remain nameless. I'd taken up my X-reg Fiesta 1100 L (I bought it thinking L stood for Loony), which I must admit doesn't look like a party leader's car. I tell salesmen it just needs a wipe over with a damp cloth, but to be honest the side looks as though somebody has emptied a Kalashnikov into it. It's not surprising it looks a bit rough as it has been parked in London streets all its life and I also use it as a convenient dumping ground for my election posters and leaflets.

On this occasion it had nevertheless got me all the

way to the by-election town as usual, and I was in my pub HQ doing a bit of campaigning at the bar when a gorgeous blonde came up and asked for some posters (quite a few people like them as they find one in the window a big deterrent to canvassers for the unofficial parties). I only had the odd badge and a few car stickers with me, so I gave her those and when she said she lived nearby I offered to drop some posters in the next day.

'Lovely,' she replied, giving me a peachy smile. 'I'll have something waiting that'll warm you up!'

Lay Down Your Arms

As I have a partner I deputed the job to Tony Dangerfield, an old mate and former bass guitar for the Savages, who had come to help canvass. Tony was unattached, so I thought him just the man to give her what she wanted. Tony used to be a smash hit with the girls when he was in the band and we used to make jokes about smuggling him into the hall under a blanket to stop him having his hair torn out by hysterical fans. He also held the band record for the most visits to the clinic afterwards, leading to his agonized claim that his bum had more holes in it than a pub dartboard.

So I ushered him on his way, telling him that if he gave her a decent seeing-to it would be worth some votes – though he hardly needed any encouragement. Tony borrowed the Fiesta and drove to her house, but the street was so packed with cars he had to park miles away and walk all the way back in his full Loony gear. By the time he reached her house the net curtains were twitching along the street and it was obvious he'd grabbed all the neighbours' attention. The blonde welcomed him at the door looking even more beautiful than ever, took him into the front room and produced coffee and biscuits. She then put on some music, sat down on the sofa beside him and pushed her chest forward. 'Will you pin my badge on?' she said softly.

One thing led to another and they were rolling about upstairs when there was a tremendous rattling on the door. 'Quick!' she said. 'That must be my husband!' The rattling below was replaced by a heavy banging.

'Christ!' Tony said. 'That bastard Sutch never told me you were married! What does your husband do?'

'He delivers concrete for paths,' she replied, looking scared.

Tony pulled on his Loony gear and was just thinking of leaping out of the window when the noise stopped, only to restart a bit of a way away. Like any nifty politician he waited for a minute before slipping downstairs and out the back to suss what was happening.

When he peeked round the side of the house he saw before him a terrible sight. A huge red-faced bloke armed with a sledgehammer was systematically destroying a yellow Cortina parked about three doors up. He'd already done the headlights and the windscreen, the grille had gone and there were massive dents in the bonnet and the front wing.

Panicking, Tony clambered over the back wall into an alley where he took off his Loony gear and stuffed it into the bag he'd been carrying the posters in. Then he emerged into the street looking just like any ordinary Joe Public. He joined the small crowd gathered to watch the auto-destruction, which was proceeding apace, and just had time to glimpse the Official Monster Raving Loony Party sticker in the back window before the sledgehammer went through it.

By then he could hear the sirens of the approaching police, so he ducked his head and sidled off to the far end of the street where he'd parked my Fiesta L. Getting in, he drove off thankfully. There was, of course, no sticker in the back window. What do you think I am – a Loony?

Great Loony Party Policies

(Those marked * have since become law)

Free skiing trips down the EEC butter mountains

Harnessing the energy of joggers by putting them on conveyor belts to generate electricity for OAPs' homes

Abolishing road tax

*Right to vote at 18

*All-day licensing for pubs

*Commercial radio

*Abolition of the 11-Plus examination

Launching a national franchise of jellied eels and tripe

Attaching all sitting MPs to a lie detector light bulb, thereby lighting up all of Westminster

Defence – all de fences will be creosoted every week to stop the other parties sitting on them

Providing free heated toilet seats for OAPs

➤

Rerouting the Channel Tunnel to the Scilly Isles, which will be renamed the Silly Isles and become an offshore tax haven

A totally free National Health Service, including prescriptions

Saving the British sausage

Putting Parliament on wheels and moving it round the country as a touring show

Trebling old-age pensions (I am getting nearer to drawing one myself)

Never mind Save the Whale – we shall introduce Save the Shrimp, you never see a whale cocktail

Reinstalling Space Hoppers as basic transport to solve the London traffic problem

Converting to EEC metric time using the 10-hour clock and thereby introducing more days to the week

Opening a National Rock Beat College

Giving votes to all family pets

Imposing a supertax on the sale of all grey suits

Swopping London Zoo with the House of Lords (and seeing if anybody notices the difference)

Moving the EEC wine lakes from France to Dartmoor to alleviate the water shortage

Filling the Dartmoor wine lakes with mackerel so they come out ready soused

Answering crucial questions like: 'Why is there only one Monopolies Commission?'

Privatizing the hot air industry so MPs' wasted breath can be sold as a heating fuel

Demoting John Major to Private

Turning Britain into Loonyland, a giant leisure park for tourists

Setting accountants in concrete and using them as traffic bollards

I'M THE LEADER
OF THE GANG, I AM

FOLLOWING THE 1987 General Election things began to look up again for Loonies in general and for us Officials in particular. The real price of the deposit was rapidly eroded by inflation and the way money was being chucked about, and the number of fringe candidates at by-elections began going up again.

Naturally I wanted to continue with my policy of standing anywhere and everywhere to spread the Loony message, but after the General Election there was an unusual gap of over a year before the next by-election in Kensington, the constituency in which I live, after which they began to come thick and fast. It is a curiosity of modern politics that the number of by-elections has been steadily decreasing over this century, partly because MPs – believe it or not – are fitter and younger. Kensington, therefore, was a welcome relief, as I was getting restless.

My main policy was to ban wheelclamping and re-employ traffic wardens as dog patrollers armed with pooper-scoopers, as I believe shovelling the shit is all they are fit for. But my by-campaign was a real disaster. I took along an Austin Princess hearse as my campaign vehicle – partly because we were dead centre of town. The vehicle was there to symbolize my pet policy at that time, which I shall introduce when I am PM, that everybody should be entitled to write

Result of Kensington By-Election, July 1988

No Vote	22,727
Dudley Fishburn (Conservative)	9829
Ann Holmes (Labour)	9014
William Goodhart (SLD)	2546
John Martin (SDP)	1190
Phylip Hobsol (Greens)	572
Cynthia Payne (Rainbow Alliance Payne and Pleasure Party)	193
Lord David Edward Sutch (OMRL)	61
John Duigan (London Class War)	60
Bryan Goodier (Anti-Left Wing Fascist)	31
Brian McDermott (Free Trade Liberal)	31
Roy Edey (Fair Wealth)	30
William Scola (Levellers)	27
John Crowley (Anti-Yuppie)	24
John Connell (Stop ITN)	20
Dr Kailish Trivedi (Independent Janata)	5
No Vote majority	12,898

down who they would vote for at the next General Election and if they die before they get a chance to vote, their written choice would stand. This would end the present injustice by which citizens kick the bucket worrying about the country falling into the wrong hands when they've gone. But the hearse proved to be a liability, first attracting a battery of parking tickets, then being wheelclamped and finally being towed away. I left it in the pound as it was not worth the cost of reclaiming it.

With the various dramas over the vehicle and my having to go to Germany for two weeks to play the Beer Palace in Berlin and Flo Circus in Hanover, I only managed a short time on the streets, where the competition was fearsome. The result was my lowest vote ever, a mere 61. However, I was delighted that Dr Kailish Trivedi of the Independent Janata party beat me hands down in the failure stakes by getting only five votes and entering the record books tied with Commander Bill Boaks. And in tribute to my Guide, once again the non-voters had triumphed by achieving a massive overall majority.

Willie and the Handjive

At Kensington I met a new candidate battling with the rules just as I had once done – Cynthia Payne. 'Madam Cyn', as she is known, is famous for having run a house of ill-repute in Streatham which accepted luncheon vouchers and her story has been made into the successful film, *Personal Services*, which stars Julie Walters.

Madam Cyn had decided to stand at Kensington as Payne and Pleasure candidate, campaigning to legalize brothels, after a friend had told her that if I could stand for Parliament, then so could she.

Madame Cyn's previous activities had given her intimate knowledge of many pillars of society, such as politicians, policemen and members of the legal and other professions, all of which stood her in good stead during her campaign.

In the Summertime

Kensington was just one of many by-elections that I contested in the last years of the '80s, and I did find they varied a lot. Some were good fun, like Fulham, where I had so many bizarrely clad Loonies on stage for the count they couldn't find the Lord Mayor. He was finally unearthed behind Leyton Summers, the Elvis Presley look-alike.

But others, like Richmond, were just dull. I made a bright start here, thinking the constituency was Richmond, London, and therefore nice and handy for me. But after two days' campaigning on the streets I met a Yorkshirewoman who told me the election was in the Richmond in her home county, where Sir Leon Brittan had vacated the seat to become a Euro-MP.

I therefore made my way north, only to find that the area had sold out to the James Herriot Country tourist bollocks. I couldn't even locate a pub which provided live entertainment for me to do a gig, although I was informed by dour locals that there was one somewhere which had a jukebox. But I couldn't find even that, and anyhow the weather was freezing, so I basically canned my whole normal campaign and didn't stay long before going back to London.

I shivered again in December when I fought Epping, promising rights for the ponies which live in the forest, and experienced the other extreme of the weather in the summer of '89, when I braved the heatwave in the inner city when standing for the Euro-election in Westminster and the Parliamentary by-election in Vauxhall on the same day.

We Loonies, unlike Mrs Thatcher, are pro-Europe,

although we have always been extremely upset about the wasteful food mountains. So for the Euro-election we derived the Euro-sausage which would use some of them up. The resulting sausage, shaped in a fashionable E-shaped logo drawn up by Sutchy and Sutchy, was launched on a Thames riverboat to the accompaniment of my old friend Mungo Jerry singing his new song written for the occasion: 'In the Sausagetime'.

There were other diversions such as the backwards walk we organized to find the silliest islander on the Scilly Isles, and which raised £2000 for CLIC, the charity devoted to helping children with leukaemia. The long walk was an epic journey which started in Sidmouth with my Monster Touring Show and the special guest star Kenny Lynch, and progressed through Devon and Cornwall to Land's End with Lord 'Tivers' Tiverton's cream Corniche cruising classily behind as support vehicle. The pilot and the stewardesses for the flight to the islands joined in the spirit of the occasion by walking backwards across the tarmac to the plane, and when we arrived on the islands we dutifully made our pilgrimage to Harold Wilson's bungalow.

We found it to be an odd little building, which the islanders rightly say looks like a shed, and unfortunately Harold was out so we could not share the bottle of Wincarnis tonic wine we had brought with us. We left it for him on the step.

In November the Berlin Wall, as I had foreseen, came down on my birthday, the tenth of November. I was very pleased about this as I know the city well after playing there many times and I knew how tense the atmosphere had been when the country had been divided. In the '60s the band's van had skidded off the icy autobahn in East Germany and rolled over the embankment. We had been rescued by a garage truck driven by a huge butch woman, who I had· joked had muscles in her spit, and we were taken off for fierce interrogation in a military barracks. Everyone there was astonished by our long hair and couldn't understand why it hadn't been cut off when we went into the army. When we told them that in Britain the army was only voluntary they simply didn't believe us.

Somehow they had got the wrecked van going though it had lost all its windows, and they give us a military escort to the border through a series of drab and grey towns. I had found it all incredibly depressing.

They Shoot Horses, Don't They?

By early 1990 I could sense that the political mood in Britain was changing and in the Mid-Staffordshire by-election in March I got a good result with 336 votes, beating five other fringe candidates, including the extremely frivolous B. Mildwater, who was campaigning to save the 2CV car which Citroën were ceasing to manufacture. Quite how even his election would prevent this happening I couldn't understand and I suspected him instead of being a plant by the sinister Dr Owen in a desperate attempt to identify possible recruits for his SDP Gang of One. This seemed quite likely as Mildwater only got 42 votes, although he did have the consolation that this was at least considerably more than the machine's brake horsepower.

More significantly, Labour won one of its greatest ever victories, turning a Tory majority of 14,654 into a Labour lead of 9449 – a swing of 21.4 per cent. The new MP, Sylvia Heal, confidently declared the result showed that 'the dark age of Thatcherism is drawing to a close'. I thought she deserved to win, partly because the Tory candidate was so poor. Throughout the years I have been standing in elections I have met a large number of prospective Parliamentary candidates, and this was yet another time when I sympathized with the voters over the lamentable choice on offer.

Candidates have always seemed to me very much of a type, and Tories in particular seem to be groomed out of the same school. They are taught to adopt a superior stance, even when they stand no chance, although over the years I have noticed their attitude to me has changed and they don't seem to look down on me as much as they did. In the early '80s particularly they constantly picked arguments with me, telling me I was making a mockery of the system and it should be left to serious people like them. I thought this extremely pompous, and a futile argument would inevitably ensue. I would tell them they had no policy for rock and rollers; they would say you can't run a country on rock and roll; I would retort it crossed all barriers; they would reply it had no depth.

None of this got anyone anywhere and I find it hard to remember which candidate said what as I have become quite muddled about them over the years. Somehow they have blurred and become all the same in my mind, with the Tories especially sporting identical neat haircuts, rosy red cheeks and blue suits as if they'd come off a conveyor belt like Barbie dolls. I call them the Porcelain Men.

Woolly Bully

At one stage I became convinced there was big deep freezer at the back of Number 10, full of Porcelain Men sitting like garden gnomes. When a by-election was announced Central Office would carry one out, put him (or her) in the back of a limo, and drive him to the constituency. By the time the Porcelain Man had been taken up the motorway with the heater on he would be thawed out and ready to go through his motions. All that was required was to give him an appropriate old school tie before you clipped the endless-loop manifesto cassette into his brain and he was off.

The Mid-Staffordshire guy was a prime Porcelain, which in turn brought another factor into the mix – this candidate himself being shoved into the background by the visiting big cheese. I went to an election meeting to see the candidate do his programmed speech, which had everybody yawning and nodding off, before he automatically asked for questions. However, these were then all answered by the visiting celeb, Kenneth Baker, who spouted the usual stock answers and bull-shit before the candidate could say anything treating him just like a dummy whose only job was to agree with the last tagline.

But I did manage to get one answer out of the actual candidate when I asked if he thought he was going to beat the Official Monster Raving Loonies. 'Yes, forty–love!' he replied on his own initiative while Baker kicked him on the shins under the table for talking out of turn.

There was another oddity at this meeting. When it

ended Baker came down the aisle and I introduced myself. 'I know you – you've stood against me,' he said. The funny thing was I never have and it was just another variation on what is always happening when politicians are on the slide. Suddenly I am getting my picture in the paper as much as them, and they rush to associate themselves with me and be at my side for photo-opportunities or any publicity.

Transfusion

Meanwhile our annual conferences at the Golden Lion continued to be successful, although after the scandals at the 1988 Olympics we had to issue a statement denying scurrilous rumours that some of our members had achieved their astonishing electoral feats by taking steroids.

The conferences were also graced by a continuous series of goodwill messages from Lord Lucan, one of our honorary members, constantly regretting he could not attend in person, while we were pleased to welcome several new potential candidates, including Baron von Thunderclap, who wished to stand as Official Monster Raving Loony Ban Volvo party. As you can imagine, all sorts of characters come to the party with their ideas, and the Baron brought along a side-angle on our battle with Dr Owen and the Gang of One with his concern about the number of road accidents involving motorbikes and Volvos. Bikers swear that the statistics prove Volvos have a higher proportion of accidents with motorbikes than any other make of car, and the Baron had been present at the historic bikers' day when two teams, armed with hacksaws, sledgehammers and oxy-acetylene cutters, got revenge by competing to be first to put an entire Volvo car through a letterbox.

I'd personally heard the same sort of thing about Volvos from a taxi-driver not long before when he had explained that because they are advertised as being the safest cars on the road, they are bought by the world's worst drivers. The trouble was, he informed me, that once installed in them these terrible drivers felt so safe they drove as if they were at the wheel of a tank. The party immediately adopted a new policy of banning all Volvos from the roads and, if that was impossible, at least forcing them to remove their bumpers. Our calculations revealed that this latter measure alone would increase available roadspace by 100 per cent.

Down Down

All this time I also followed Dr David Owen's changing fortunes with great interest. The Alliance had now become the SLD – the Social Liberal Democrats – although I called it the Sutch Lord David party. But Owen had refused to merge the remnants of his SDP with the Liberals, and when we invited him to merge with us instead he churlishly, and with typical arrogance, refused. It was then I made my decision that if he would not take the olive branch we were so graciously holding out to him, we should instead move to crush him. And on 25 May 1990, when the returning officer shuffled forward to announce the result of the Bootle by-election, I demonstrated how effectively I had done precisely that.

The foundations of Owen's demise had been laid

earlier that year when I bumped into my old friend Tony King when I was playing Butlin's in Ayr. I'd known Tony in the old days of the Cavern when he played bass for one of the Merseybeat bands, and had seen both him and his wife Val on and off over the years. As we got chatting over a few pints Tony now explained he was running an entertainment agency just down the road from Bootle in Liverpool.

He then offered not just to be my agent at the by-election, but actually to organize my campaign. The notion of any sort of organization was a dizzying prospect, and one which might break me out of my plastic-bag culture and shatter a sacred tenet of Loonyism. But Tony persuaded me that for once the party could be serious about its campaign – or at least as serious as it was able.

With a Little Help From My Friends

The strategy we hammered out was for me to stand as Official Monster Raving Loony Cavern Rock party to stress local issues. I was disgusted by the new plastic 'Beatles Story' exhibition set up in the trendy Albert Dock, while the original Cavern had been filled in to make a car park, and I therefore pledged to rebuild it. To further cheer up people – and they certainly need cheering up in Bootle – I promised to turn the town into an independent state; revive the old Overhead railway; provide heated toilet seats for old age pensioners, and introduce PRAT – the People's Retrospective Allowance Tax which was our sensible answer to the Poll Tax.

Then, thanks to Tony, for the first time I had state

of the art technology putting me on equal terms with the unofficial parties with a computer, fax, and always-available phone number. Like them I now started peppering the media with press releases and photo-opportunities and the result was to prove devastating.

Lily the Pink

At the beginning of the campaign I assessed our chances of beating Owen's candidate as only marginal. We knew that the SDP was in serious trouble and that now that Owen had refused to join the merged SLD he only had two MPs left. I had also watched the SDP lose its deposit in the two preceding by-elections, with a particularly poor show at Mid-Staffs, where it only got 1422 votes. But I still had to face the fact the SDP was a major unofficial party, while we were only Official Loonies, and the revised boundary for Bootle now included part of the old Crosby constituency which Shirley Williams had won in the SDP heyday in 1981. Some of her supporters must still be alive and driving around in their Volvos, even if they had stopped their credit card subscriptions to the party.

But I drew courage from being back near my old stamping ground of Huyton, where I had succeeded against Harold and received the talisman of the Winston cigar, and as my campaign got into gear I sensed a Loony surge amongst Bootleans. The people warmed especially to my innovative plan to make Ken Dodd Chancellor of the Exchequer as he was a local hero after successfully fighting off income tax charges. (I'd also decided Arthur Scargill, after his brilliant handling of

the funds in the miners' strike, should be made First
Lord of the Treasury.)

I set up my party headquarters in Addison's Wine
Bar in the heart of town where the manager, Dave
Holmes, gave me all the facilities I needed to go out
on to the streets with Tony's band, the Undertakers,
another '60s legacy. I used them to campaign in funereal
garb, carrying a white coffin with 'Kill the Poll Tax'
written on it. When the lid was opened a hand emerged
to dispense our new Loony money – Bank of Loonyland
notes bearing Thatcher's head and stating 'I promise
the cheque is in the post'. The notes paid 1lb of flesh
and were tremendously popular.

Seeing how well we were doing, I suspected the
worst when two smiling high-ranking police officers
walked into Addison's just as Granada TV was about
to film the Undertakers on their coffinabout. In front of
the astonished crew the law informed me I was breaking the Representation of the People Act by having my
campaign headquarters on licensed premises.

I knew we were in a dirty campaign when they
further told me it was the Labour party which had
made the complaint after our big banner had been
seen outside. But the complaint rebounded badly when
the story catapulted on to the front page, castigating
Labour under the headline KINNOCK'S KILLJOYS, and from
then on we never looked back.

As usual I was holding my victory party the night
before polling and I arrived at Lime Street station
to be confronted by Dr Owen and his candidate,
who grinned mockingly at me. I went up and shook
them both by the hand and invited the leader to
my party.

'I'd really love to come,' Owen replied, sighing

deeply. 'I can see it would be a lot of fun, but I've got to go. Maybe next time.'

But there was never to be a next time, and Owen did indeed miss a good party. More than fifteen hundred people packed into the wine bar and I performed my rock'n'politics show to tumultuous applause.

Such a Night

The count was at Bootle town hall, a typically northern Gothic monolith, and as I went in I met the Chief Constable, who confessed the police had found their reference books to be five years out of date. I hadn't been committing an electoral offence by using the wine bar he now told me and I accepted his apology with good grace and autographed some Loony money for him at his request before I moved on to the serious business of the evening.

From the looks we were getting it was clear my spookily dressed Undertakers and I were an unaccustomed sight, even though the full effect had been spoilt by their being made to leave the coffin outside. The atmosphere in the town hall was electric, but the true excitement began when people saw the wooden tray containing Loony votes was filling up faster than the one for the SDP. Halfway through the count I was well into the lead, which I found hard to believe after being dazzled by the charismatic doctor himself the previous night.

But my eyes had not been deceiving me and at the end of the count my votes totalled 418 – a staggering 1.2 per cent of the poll. In contrast Jack Holmes, the SDP candidate, had obtained a paltry 155, which is o.4 per cent! Unofficially my non-voting supporters also did me proud by registering a massive 49.8 per cent – a result which my Guide, Commander Boaks, would have been thrilled by.

Let's Have a Party

The second the newly elected Labour candidate had finished his photo-call the TV cameras zoomed in on me. 'What went wrong?' the interviewer asked. For once I was lost for words, the shock was so great. 'We had a great campaign,' I replied rather feebly. 'It just goes to show what rock and roll can do for politics.' The interviewer trumpeted on, telling viewers what I already knew. The OMRLP had smashed the party which had promised to break the mould of British politics but, as I'd always predicted, hadn't been able to handle the blancmange of success.

My supporters were ecstatic and the next morning the papers were full of Owen's humiliation, while in the Commons there was huge merriment as Labour MP Tony Banks asked the Speaker to call 'Screaming Lord Owen'. I felt even prouder when shortly afterwards Owen announced his decision to wind up the SDP, openly admitting that its trouncing at our hands had been a deciding factor.

Two weeks later, in the dimly lit Boardroom One of the St James's Court Hotel, just round the corner from Buckingham Palace, the formal end came when the SDP national committee voted 17 to 5 to call it a day. It was an undignifed final performance with the usual squabbling in the ranks and some members still loonily insisting the party had a future – even though

---

Result of the Bootle By-Election

No Vote	35,194
Michael Carr (Labour)	26,737
James Clappison (Conservative)	3220
John Cunningham (Liberal Democrat)	3179
S. Brady (Green)	1267
K. White (Liberal)	474
Lord David Edward Sutch (Official Monster Raving Loony Cavern Rock party)	418
Jack Holmes (SDP)	155
Timothy Schofield (Independent)	27
No Vote majority	8457

---

the opinion polls showed it down to 1 per cent. One member even accused Owen of engineering the end of the party as a 'get out' so he could work his way back into the Labour party, although they would hardly want him back after he'd been finished off by me.

Combine Harvester (Brand New Key)

Following this triumph I decided it was time for a new push and instructed Sutchy and Sutchy to come up with an ecologically sound ad campaign reinforcing our commitment to the '90s. Their clever idea was corn circles, which our agents then created all over southern England. What was most brilliant about the strategy was virtually no one realized we were responsible and there was a rash of fanciful theories which went as far as creatures from outer space, although presumably to the disappointment of the Loony Posadists, who had supported Wedgwood Benn, they had not brought socialism with them. (Out of interest I can now reveal the corn circles were created by using the backwash from a Marshall amplifier.)

There were other circles for me that autumn. Cliff Richard, who has gone a long way on the back of being a good-looking guy, had just celebrated his fiftieth birthday by boasting he didn't drink, smoke or sleep with girls. I reckoned the true position was that he'd been dead for the last ten years but nobody had got round to telling him.

Now it was my time to face the big Five-Oh myself and I celebrated this milestone with a bash at the Wall Street club in Bruton Place WI, where much of the filming was done for *Scandal*, the film about the Profumo Affair. I had been to the premiere and the celebratory party afterwards at the Liberal club, where I'd met Christine Keeler. I told her she was the reason I'd gone into politics in the first place to which she replied, putting her hand up to her face, 'Oh dear. Now that's another thing they'll blame me for!'

The party was a really wild and boozy affair, with an astonishing number of beautiful women, and went on until five in the morning. I found it really bizarre contrasting the stern figures of past Liberal worthies scowling down at such a drunken rabble and it occurred to me that the political editor of *Sunday Sport* must have dropped in as some of the girls were kissing the statues and hanging round their necks. I saw one of them bare her breasts at one, saying: 'Get a butchers of these, you miserable-looking old bugger,' and joined in the fun by putting my top hat and a 'Vote Raving Loony' sticker on Gladstone, with another on his bag for good measure.

I Can See Clearly Now

My own birthday celebration was more civilized, with old mates like Jet Harris of the Shadows, Graham Fenton of Matchbox, Mungo Jerry, Joe Brown, and Chas Hodges of Chas and Dave. Quite frankly I was amazed to still be here, rocking and rolling and doing '50s songs when I was fifty myself. But music had kept me in touch with the younger generation and the way they were thinking, and I concluded I must still be a kid at heart.

Anyhow, politically I was just coming into my prime. Having crossed the fifty barrier, and been approved of by Bernard Levin in a large piece in *The Times*, there seemed no reason why, just like Mrs Thatcher was stating she would, I couldn't go on and on for ever. But whether Thatcher could was a different matter. The image-makers had to run out of ideas one day, and Saatchi and Saatchi's share price had gone through the floor as the City and the Yuppie market crashed. (Sutchy and Sutchy of course remained buoyant.)

Nigel Lawson and Lord Young had cleared off to make fortunes in the City, Nicholas Ridley had got the push for slagging off the Krauts, Edwina Currie had eggcelled herself and been scrambled, and now the Iron Lady herself was beginning to look very rusty and in need of a good oiling. But at that moment little did I realize the crucial part I was destined to play in bringing about her downfall.

WAKE UP, MAGGIE

I DID not directly set in train the events which unseated Margaret Thatcher. I had more important things to do, like playing Napoleon's in Openshawe, Manchester, under the auspices of its popular compere, Larry 'Teapot' Richards. More and more I seemed to have been sacrificing my rock and roll for politics and now I had Dr Death's scalp dangling from my belt I felt ready for a crack at another big target. So when the Tory party handed me my chance I seized it without hesitation. In doing so of course I changed the course of history but that, as Winston had told me when he marked me out, is what I am here for.

I had seen how, as the recession loomed ever closer, the papers and TV had turned against Thatcher and accused her of being out of touch. There had been some rumblings about her at the 1990 OMRLP conference in October, which had unilaterally voted to demote John Major to Private for his handling of the economy.

Everybody was moaning about how broke they were and several party members crept up to me at the bar and pleaded with me to get rid of her. Someone was going to have to give her a push and I was the man for the job, they all told me. As they were all Loonies I largely discounted that. But when I was monitoring the Tory party conference a couple of weeks later I was reminded how isolated Maggie was from the average voter – and especially the average non-voter whose interests I had most at heart.

Bird Dog

As part of their rubbishing of Paddy Ashdown's SLD – surging ahead now Owen had crumbled – her speech-writers had likened its silly new logo to the Monty Python dead parrot comedy sketch, which must be about the best-known in Britain. Yet Maggie, completely puzzled, had never even heard of it. Maybe, I thought, it was time I did something. My Tory moles were moaning that Thatcher was so OTT a rumour was circulating that she'd defected to us. I immediately ordered a rigorous search of party files and there was near panic when one of my minions, double-checking under Thatcher's maiden name of Roberts (you can't be too careful with these people), found a K. Roberts in Southgate, suspiciously close to Finchley.

Fortunately I was able to reassure anxious followers this was just my old friend Kim Roberts, whose impeccable Loony credentials were proved by owning Splodge, a small terrier who is our Hon Member for Barking. But the membership was still jittery, worried that extremists might be infiltrating the party once again.

It was shortly after this, as I watched Geoffrey 'Howe's That' Howe's dramatic resignation speech, I realized none of the original 1979 Cabinet nuts were left and it would obviously soon fall apart. At Ashburton we'd found Howe even less savage than the dead sheep Denis Healey had called him. More like a worm, we'd concluded. Now even the worm had turned against her.

Out of Time

I knew straight away Mike Heseltine would be swinging into action. Since he'd called me in as a consultant I'd only come across him once, when he visited Kensington to support the Tory candidate in the 1988 by-election. Seeing one of my punky followers wearing a topper he asked for me, but as I was a few streets away rattling letterboxes I missed him. Instead I got a message reading: 'Rubberneck Roadshow going fab. Blue-rinsers on board. Book reprinting. Wilco and out.' By now he had hawked his act round the country so that huge numbers of Tories shared his personal opinion he was Maggie's natural successor.

When Heseltine phoned immediately after Howe's resignation I took the opportunity of reminding him of Sutchy and Sutchy's unpaid bill. 'I told you gentlemen never discuss money,' he yelled back. 'See my man some time. Meanwhile I'm ringing, you Loony, to see if the time is right. The old roadshow has been dead gear and everyone's raved about it, but I told everybody I'd be Prime Minister, and I'm already fifty-seven. So, Dave, do I go for it now?'

'Yep,' I replied without hesitation. 'Howe's done the work for you in splitting the Cabinet, so get your nasty little chopper out and do your worst.' But I did think I should add a word of warning: 'Mikey baby, you must get into this cricketing stuff,' I advised him. 'Maggie's saying she'll field the bouncers, Howe's moaning his bat's been broken by the team captain, so you need something to do with cricket in it as well. How about changing your name to Buddy Holly? He's due for another revival.'

'Don't be a bloody Loony!' he snapped back. 'This is politics, dammit, not some stupid game.'

'OK, Mike,' I replied. 'The others don't seem to think so. But as you already talk a load of balls I suppose you're halfway there without trying. But you'll still have some major hurdles to overcome before you bowl the Iron Maiden out.'

'Easy-peasy!' was the wild cry from the other end. 'I've always been good at the jumps – even if I can't match old Parky at that game. Oo-ee-eeu! Oo-ee-eeu! Over and out!'

Three Steps to Heaven

Monitoring the TV activity a few days later I listened incredulous as a Man in a Suit explained the Tory party rules for the coming leadership contest and they seemed even more Loony than the Loony party! For a start they stated that the contest could be held to challenge a sitting Prime Minister – something I, as a fellow party leader, would never allow. Then to win in the first ballot you needed 55 per cent of the votes, which was more Loony logic. The other fight game I knew, boxing, was governed by the Queensberry rules, which were much more sensible as well as having a better pedigree. In boxing you could win by a single point on a split decision. But looniest of all, not just MPs but any member of the Conservative party could stand. As a mole told me, cabals plotting in the House of Commons tearoom were now openly referring to

the 'Conservative and Loonyist party'. Having such
Loony rules of course put the Tories squarely in my
territory. Worst of all, the way things were going
there might even be a 'Bring back Ted Heath – all is
forgiven' movement developing – and that would even
be without the Band, which had split up years ago.

And weighing on my leopardskin shoulders I also
felt the weight of my responsibility to the non-voters
of Britain. Some Tory MPs would obviously want to
mirror the population by not voting – which they
could do in this case by abstaining. The proportion
was bound to be lower than in the electorate as a
whole, as MPs had to be keen on voting to get their
jobs in the first place. But there would still be potential
abstainers needing a flag to rally round. My duty to
them was clear.

I Hear You Knocking

After long consultations at the bar of the Golden Lion
I determined to throw my hat into the ring. (That was
another point confirming my right to stand. With my
faithful topper, I seemed to be the only politician these
days with a hat to throw.) Returning to my London HQ
I took the short taxi ride to the Kensington and Chelsea
Conservative Association. I found its premises located
in a basement, which amply confirmed the impression
of skulduggery below stairs characterizing the party at
the time.

I was greeted by a pleasant, quite ordinary-looking
woman who smiled and said, 'We've been expecting you, sir,' before she took me into a murky back
room and asked for a donation. I handed over a

£10 note and was given a blue membership card in return.

'That'll do nicely, ma'am!' I quipped, declining her offer to subscribe to the monthly 'Conservative Newsline' newspaper unless I was put on the front page.

Glancing through the programme of events she handed me I saw the Association was about to hold its annual ball with the star attraction being Douglas Hurd. The only musical role I could imagine for Hitler Hurd, as he was known at school, was being a roadie for the Osmonds. I realized he'd be so tedious they'd end up playing Neighbourhood Watch so magnanimously I offered the services of myself and the Savages to liven things up. The woman did not appear to have heard of us, but listened politely as I explained our act. To make it clearer to her I told her that it was the sort of music Geoffrey Howe would hate, which cheered her up immensely. She did promise to have a word with the committee, but there must have been some communications failure, as she never came back to confirm the gig.

You'll Never Walk Alone

Now I was a member of the Tory party I set about undermining Maggie from within. Taking full advantage of the Loony rules, I publicly announced I would stand in competition with Heseltine and the Heselteenies. I broke the news in the Peterborough diary column of the *Daily Telegraph*, which I always think is the surest route to old-fashioned Tory MPs, as it is the paper said to be read by the people who think they run the country.

At this stage few MPs had the nous to realize that Maggie was in danger, so I didn't expect any public pledges of support. I needed the backing of two sitting MPs to get on the ballot sheet, but the closet Loonies in the party were too cowed by the atmosphere of terror at Westminster to put their heads above the parapet. One or two of the more honest ones muttered their only concern was saving their own skins. Maggie might be awful, they moaned, but Heseltine was an even bigger shit.

When I rang them at home they were no better, cursing me as they furtively whispered their phones were being bugged by MI5 on Maggie's orders. Thinking this was probably true, for a bit of fun I rang a few I especially disliked and pretended to be very matey. But strictly off the record, as the hacks say, it was a different matter. Oblique messages of support reached me from MPs promising to emulate my non-voters by abstaining. I could see why as I sat in my front room monitoring the TV coverage and saw how they were slagging each other off in public. It was obvious they had all been well trained in the art at their public schools, and you could spot the bullies a mile off.

But I still thought Maggie could handle it until I saw she was going to Paris to boast to the rest of Europe how she had ended the Cold War. As far as I and everybody I knew was concerned, that had been over for years anyway. We musicians always have great faith in our ability to cross frontiers, and I sincerely believe the spread of Western pop music helped to break down the barriers between East and West. I have met quite a few Russians, all of whom knew my records from tapes taken from Finnish radio stations.

Singers like Elton John, who went long before

Thatcher described Gorbachev as 'a man I could do business with', made huge breakthroughs with ordinary people. I will never forget a Russian singer who came over after *glasnost* telling me in all seriousness: 'How could we possibly fight with Britain after the Beatles had made "Back in the USSR"?'

The First Cut is the Deepest

Although Maggie and her inept campaign managers could obviously not see it, I knew that once she was out of the way my Commons mice would be encouraged to play. Sure enough, as soon as she had departed I got the promises of some forty MPs – possibly enough to give me the balance of power. The actual ballot proved most of them had been lying, though as that is their profession, this was hardly surprising. However, a plucky sixteen had stuck by their guns and tipped the balance. Maggie scored more than half the votes, but thanks to my abstainers, not the 206 she needed for the 55 per cent majority required by the Loony rules.

Instead she fell just two short with 204, whilst the Heseltine Rubberneck Roadshow pulled a respectable 152. If only two of my supporters had switched to her, she would have been home and dry . . .

You Can't Hurry Love

When I saw Maggie live on TV from Paris, declaring she was standing for the second round without even consulting her campaign managers, I knew I'd been right to intervene. But what should I do next?

Fortunately she solved my dilemma for me by acknowledging she would lose against Heseltine and tearfully withdrawing from the contest. I was driving through Brixton in the Fiesta Loony at the time and caught the end of the newsflash as I switched on the radio. But I thought it was something like Roy Hudd's Huddlines until I got back to my HQ and saw on TV that it was official. The news immediately explained the odd things I'd seen in the streets. Pedestrians had been dancing with joy whilst drivers hooted their horns with elation and all the cars flashed their lights. There had even been the rarest thing it is possible to see in the capital – taxi-drivers actually grinning and looking happy.

I made a cup of tea, putting in an unaccustomed dash of whisky as the full enormity of what I had done sank in. I and my faithful Tory closet Loonies had done what the Labour party had failed to do in eleven and a half years and brought the final curtain down on the Iron Lady.

As I'd half expected, the phone started ringing itself off the hook. I picked it up, expecting the national papers wanting a comment. 'You bloody idiot, look what you've done now!' a familiar voice screamed. 'That pipsqueak goody-goody Major and that old fart Hurd have joined the stampede for my job. Don't you realize this means real competition – some of the Cabinet actually go as far as liking these people!'

'It's not my fault,' I replied, tersely reminding him about Sutchy and Sutchy's unpaid invoice.

'The cheque's in the post, you bloody Loony,' he shouted back. 'You got me into this mess – now get me out!'

By now Heseltine was beginning to get on my wick,

as he was apparently getting on everybody else's. 'Why not turn out a quick rap record like Gazza,' I advised him in a bored fashion. 'He's just like you – can't sing a note either. But he's still got to Number Two in the charts. All the papers are calling you "Hezza", so you should at least pick up some sales from morons getting the two of you muddled up.'

The voice at the other end went incoherent with rage. 'I'll get you for this, you Loony bastard!' Heseltine shouted, slamming down the phone. I switched on the answering machine so as not to be disturbed further and turned my attention back to the TV to weigh up his new competition.

Major to Minor

Hurd, the star of the Kensington Association Ball, was obviously a joke, striking me as a cross between Elton John's dad and one of the Woodentops. But Major was a different matter. I'd come across him in the distant past just before I went into rock and roll and was putting a bit of bread together on a building site. John had been my hod carrier taking mortar to the brickies, and although he was fresh out of school it was already clear he was too delicate and studious to do anything you could call proper work.

One morning during a teabreak, as he fussed about getting his hands dirty and painstakingly wiped the brick dust off his specs, I told him he'd be much happier behind a desk.

'Accountancy's more your bag, man,' I informed him. 'Why not nip off to John Collier's – the window to watch – and buy yourself a nifty grey suit. Then start banging on a few bank doors.'

He frowned in a concerned fashion as he carefully considered this. 'Are you quite sure that's a good idea, David?' he ventured hesitantly. 'You see, I'd been thinking accountancy might be too exciting for me. I'm told it can be rather dramatic.' Looking crestfallen, he then stared at the ground in embarrassment. 'Anyhow, I'm not awfully good at sums,' he finally confessed.

'Suit yourself,' I replied offhandedly, knowing the pun would go straight over his head. Like the other blokes on the site I was quickly bored by him. The last I had heard before he disappeared off my map was he'd gone to be a bus conductor but failed the test. Now here he was on the box, still blinking through his specs, wearing the suit, and running for Prime Minister. If he wasn't adjudged fit to gather bus fares, I didn't see how he could be thought fit to run the country – but that's politics for you.

Get Off My Cloud

With this latest development my closet Loony MPs – the plucky sixteen abstainers – were beside themselves with agitation. None, fortunately for them, had so far been unmasked and I will not break faith now by revealing their true identities. Suffice it to say they are all smug bastards living in big houses whose motto is: 'I'm all right, Jack' – a description which will assure their anonymity.

'Come out,' I advised one as he panicked away to me on his carphone. 'Cross the House to the Loonies

– you might as well after the shambles you've all made of the Conservative party.'

'No! No!' the petrified voice replied. 'Maggie's told us we've all to grow up and pull ourselves together. All hell's broken loose in Smith Square and constituency members are threatening to resign left, right and centre. Even Bernard Ingham can't muzzle the press on this one!'

I sighed with despair. There was no need to panic just because the public was seeing the wheels go round. Nothing had surprised us Loonies. I was tiring of these pinheads with their minuscule grasp of the punters' thinking, so I made a quick sounding of OMRLP members and unanimously they agreed that we should drop the lot of them.

'Take your wife's advice,' I told the next one who rang, 'then at least you'll get some peace at home.' (Mind you, I thought, if John Major had taken Norma's advice he'd never have stood in the first place.)

In the second ballot, as I knew he would, Major put his snotty nose ahead, Hurd was nowhere and Hezza, with no rap record to boost his chances, actually got less votes than in the first round. But just like Maggie, Major was two short of the overall majority he needed.

In theory there should have been a third ballot, but like true politicians Hurd and Heseltine instantly caved in and withdrew to curry favour with the new boss. The Loonies running the party then changed the rules yet again, scrubbed the third ballot and declared Major elected. The result at the end of the day was therefore Major becoming Prime Minister with 185 votes, whilst Maggie, with 204, lost the job. If I ever needed proof the Tories were more Loony than us, there it was in black and white.

I Who Have Nothing

I sent Heseltine a brief fax reading: 'Congratulations Hezza on joining Gazza in the losers' club.' I knew he really had nothing to worry about and after the result he'd said himself: 'Another day dawns.' He was right.

I couldn't see him crying like Gazza, though Mrs H looked a teeny bit tearful on TV. But I was sure some of the Heselteenies were weeping buckets, especially as they knew they were certain to be punished for the most serious Tory crime of all – backing a loser. But like Gazza I wanted Heseltine to uphold the age-old British tradition of being more successful by losing than winning. I'd tried to explain this to my old friend Rodney Bingenheimer when he'd breezed into town from LA a couple of months previously and we'd had a meet at Stringfellow's, the famous night club in the West End.

Peter Stringfellow is a good friend of mine and our association goes back to his roots in Sheffield, when I was the first professional act at his Black Cat club, which started in a church hall he hired for ten shillings a night. Peter was panicking at the thought of filling it, but it proved a sell-out, and from then on he never looked back. I became a regular performer there and was the first band to play live at the old Talk of the Town in Leicester Square which he later reopened as the Hippodrome. We have a lot of common ground from our past and have kept in touch, and he is a great Raving Loony supporter.

'What's all this Gazza shit I see everywhere,' Bingenheimer demanded as we elbowed a couple of minor celebs out of their seats. 'Who is he and what's he done?'.

'You won't believe this,' I replied. 'He's making millions . . .'

'I know that,' Bingenheimer interrupted. 'Cut the crap, man. Just tell me what the big deal is.'

'Well, Gazza's a footballer who played in the World Cup,' I explained. 'And he and his team got beaten in the quarter final by the Germans.'

'So what did he do to be so famous?' Bingenheimer demanded impatiently. 'Shoot the German captain?'

'Nothing like that,' I replied. 'Just like a spoilt child, he started to cry. I mean, really cry – not the normal hype. The tears were flooding down his face.'

'So?' Bingenheimer snapped.

'That's it,' I concluded, and Bingenheimer shook his head, as mystified by the doings of the Brits as ever. We'd had the same trouble the previous time he'd been over and found Frank Bruno hailed as a hero, even though he had just been flattened by Mike Tyson in the World Heavyweight Championship. In Bingenheimer's West Coast world – as I'd found out when I was over there – you're either the winner, or you're dead.

'It's just like Bruno all over again,' I tried to explain. 'Gazza's another loser, who by losing has won in the end, because it's made him a millionaire.'

Bingenheimer looked at me craftily. 'So if I kick you in the balls, that'll make us both rich?' he enquired.

'It's more complicated than that,' I sighed, knowing that, like Hezza, he would never understand.

I Got You, Babe

Looking back, I still have mixed feelings about deposing Maggie. But Major did introduce one plus for the lads by keeping women out of his Cabinet. Now the men wouldn't have to keep on putting the seat back down on the Cabinet lavatory, which I saw as a special bonus for the Wets as their aim was so bad.

Maggie was the fourth Tory leader I'd seen off and I knew she would fade away as quickly as the Ted Heath Band. But in some ways I was sad to see her go as at least she'd shared my objective of bringing some colour into politics. I'll always remember seeing her on TV just before Major emerged from the door of Number 10 as Prime Minister for the first time. She was hovering behind the net curtains on the first floor, for once unsure whether she was on camera or off, but smiling just in case. Some people never give up.

But she thought then she had plenty of reason to be satisfied, as Major was her choice as successor and she'd already told everybody she'd be the back-seat driver. Denis, who I saw grumpily loading his golf clubs into a battered old Mark III Cortina, knew full well what that meant. And Maggie did get the consolation prize from the Queen of being made a member of the exclusive Order of Merit, just as Churchill had been on his retirement. When I heard the news I wondered how long it was since she had last worn a garter – or if Denis, now a hereditary baronet, had ever worn one in his life. It was a gruesome thought.

But now that the couple were to have more time

together in their Dulwich home I was sure they would remember our local Loony slogan for the constituency: 'More Dick in Dulwich!' From my sofa in front of the TV I exhorted Denis to go for it before, exhausted by all the drama, I blanked the TV and made a pot of PG Tips.

As I sipped it I looked fondly at my battered old Lurex leopardskin lying on the sofa. Major's central message was the triumph of the Men in Grey Suits and I could see him pinning on his apron and donning his rubber gloves to do the washing up as he proudly droned on to Norma about his first day as PM. As I imagined his nasal pedantic voice going on, I was irresistibly reminded of a voice I had heard somewhere in the past. Then I remembered – the trainspotters on the bridge at Crewe station! I could just hear Major: 'Of course that's the old London and Midland livery which strictly speaking was abolished with nationalization in 1948, with the exception of certain members classified . . .'

I shifted my gaze to Churchill's portrait on the wall as I mused on how the papers and the TV were hyping this dull grey person as 'the man of the people' and representative of the classless society. I believe I saw Winnie give me a wink and we were sharing a wry smile when our ruminations were rudely shattered by the phone.

'A by-election's been announced in Ribble Valley,' a reporter from the *Burnley Advertiser* was shouting excitedly. 'Will you be standing?'

Would I indeed! The time had come for me to move seamlessly towards my most glorious election triumph of all. After thirty years I was to finally overtake my Guide, the late, great Commander Bill Boaks, to become Britain's most successful Parliamentary candidate by standing for Parliament more times than anyone else. As Boaks was dead and there was no opposition anywhere in sight, my rightful place in British political history was now assured. But before that I had a last pilgrimage to make – from Napoleon's in Openshawe to Downing Street to witness Maggie's last curtain call.

I'm Left, You're Right, She's Gone

On the train from Manchester I noticed there was already a different atmosphere as the buffet staff, thinking themselves free of the threat of privatization, rejoiced in being surly again. Even the sandwiches seemed to have readopted their old derisive sneers as they curled at the edges and I made a mental note to try out the new flavours on our mascot the Loch Ness Monster. I feed them to it regularly in the constant hope that it will be so disgusted it will one day surface to throw them back, at which point I will throw a net over it. So far this ploy has failed, and I have informed the Scottish press I have a horrible suspicion that Cyril Smith has already eaten Nessie.

Arriving at the Commons, I saw about two hundred people in white coats milling around on the green outside. I presumed they had been called to take away Tory MPs demented by the crisis until they revealed themselves as jam tart-makers protesting about new Euro legislation. I had to feel sorry for their timing – the Queen of Hearts would be making no tarts that day.

Abandoning them to their fate, I walked up Whitehall to stand outside the security gates at the end of Downing Street which were another grim legacy of the Thatcher years. To pass the time I scanned the paper, reading that Denis had stopped that morning to exchange his first words with the roadsweeper since he and Maggie had moved in. Times were obviously changing fast.

The policemen on duty were as friendly as ever, asking for Recycled Loony Teenager badges and letting me stand in front of the crash barriers for a TV interview. All the people around said they would vote for me. 'The real lunatics come in and out of there,' one remarked darkly, nodding towards the black door of Number 10. I swallowed the insult manfully.

At 2.20 p.m. Maggie emerged wearing a dark blue suit with white braid and stepped into the Jaguar to be driven to her last Prime Minister's Question Time. As she swept past with her nose in the air and a stunned, frozen look on her face, I doffed my topper courteously and turned away.

It was, as all the papers were saying, the end of an era. Maggie, obviously completely zonked by the turn of events, marked her passing by saying, 'It's a funny old world'. I wasn't surprised she was puzzled. She had been the most unfunny of the lot of them.

It was time to move on. Picking up my plastic bag I headed for Euston, passing a souvenir shop where they were already taking down Maggie masks. I rushed in to buy one cheap, only to be rebuffed by the owner. 'We're only doing it as a photo-opportunity for the press, then we're putting them back at full price,' he told me smugly, adding: 'You see, squire, now she's gone they've become collectors' items. So they're worth more now, aren't they, guv?'

Cursing Maggie for her popular capitalism and the way it had perverted the minds of small shopkeepers, I threaded my way past the beggars and shook the dust of the capital from my feet.

KING OF THE ROAD

LIKE MANY other people, I entered the New Year of 1991 apprehensively with the prospect of the imminent Gulf war perpetrated by the tinpot dictator Saddam Hussein. We regarded him as too Loony to even be in the Loony party. On occasions like this, when people's lives are at stake, we Loonies hang back, so I turned my attention to reviewing the position at home where the Poll Tax and the new Business Rates were wreaking havoc. Major was faithfully following in Maggie's footsteps and refusing to cut interest rates and businesses were crashing left, right and centre.

Christmas had been a wash-out in the shops and I wondered what Winston would have made of the world the unofficial parties had created. I imagined him surveying the welter of HP repayments, mortgages, bank loans and exorbitant credit now oppressing the British people. 'Never in the field of human conflict,' he would be growling, 'has so much been owed by so many to so few . . .'

What with the war, the horrid sideshow of Gorbachev using the Gulf to crack down on the Russian satellite states, freezing weather, and the collapse of British Rail I felt the population seriously needed cheering up. I did my best at Ribble Valley, which is just off the M6 at Preston, Lancashire. The constituency was one of the Tories' ten safest seats in the land and had been held by David Waddington, an undistinguished Home Secretary who had now been made a lord.

Although for me Ribble was to be the scene of my greatest triumph as I overtook Commander Boaks, during the actual campaigning this, along with everything else, was thrust aside by the massive furore about the Poll Tax which was the only election issue. Naturally I had been against it since the start and when Michael Heseltine arrived to support the Tory candidate I sympathized with him for being handed the poisoned chalice of having to sort it out on his return to the Tory Cabinet.

'Scrap the tax, man,' I told him. 'It's the only thing you can do.'

'Piss off, will you,' he hissed back at me. 'You've already wrecked my career with that bloody Rubberneck Roadshow. The last thing I need now is another of your Loony ideas.'

'Come on, Mikey, you know it makes sense,' I chided him. 'After all, you're the one who'll do anything to get elected – so you don't need to bother about principles, do you, eh?' Heseltine just glared at me and went off to coiffure his mane prior to giving his speech, and of course later he did take my advice once again. I did however notice that the news the Poll Tax was to be scrapped was conveniently timed to defuse publicity for the release of the Birmingham Six – an episode which I, like many other Britons, feel very ashamed of.

But at the time of Ribble Valley the Poll Tax was still in place, and I was privileged to witness the awesome sight of the Tory shires in revolt. The Conservatives were so desperate they even wheeled in Jeffrey Archer, who I watched going to great lengths to avoid being photographed with Lindi St Clair, the saucy Miss Whiplash who stands for the Corrective party.

I did the Undertakers thing again with the coffin, and Tony King, who had organized my Bootle triumph over Dr Owen, helped me get together a manifesto featuring promises to build Loonyland in the constituency and hold a massive annual music festival. But nobody was interested and all I got was a stream of angry Tories telling me they would be voting Liberal Democrat – which they did with a vengeance, demoting their own party to a poor second place.

Much more significantly, I scored a respectable 278 votes to achieve my long-awaited and hard-earned objective and the newspapers proclaimed how I had now stood in more than thirty elections, overtaking Commander Boaks to take my rightful place in the hall of fame. In many ways it was the climax of my political career. I already knew there was a slight problem in my claiming the record as Boaks himself had not been sure of precisely how many times he had stood. Thirty had just been his guesstimate, but it sounded about right to me, and I was just about to start planning a monster celebration when Peter, the person so kindly helping me pen these memoirs, whispered in my ear.

'David, never mind old Boaksy, I can't work out precisely how many elections you've stood in either,' he told me and I felt a momentary pang of pity as I recalled him endlessly toiling through mounds of my plastic bags in search of elusive hard facts amongst the dross of newspaper cuttings.

'What exactly do you mean?' I asked carefully.

'Well, David, I don't know how to put this,' he replied. 'There's no doubt you've stood in an awful lot of by-elections. It is definitely over twenty-five and it may well be thirty, but I can't be sure. And, to be perfectly honest, your stuff's in such a mess I don't think I'll ever be able to work it out precisely.'

I looked at him as he sat hollow-eyed and exhausted amongst the contents of the turned-out bags. The poor man had done his best, and what he was saying was probably true. Anyway, I was tickled by the thought of both contestants for the Loony record not knowing exactly where they were. Somehow it was appropriate. And I recalled another occasion when I'd learnt the hard way that sometimes it was better to be content with what you'd got than to push things too much, and I now told him the story.

Hello Goodbye

I was once walking through a street market in Nottingham on a miserable day, so muffled up against the cold you could hardy see my face and wearing ordinary clothes. I knew nobody could recognize me.

I stopped to chat to the guy on the record collector's stall and he started going on about how my records were real rarities and yet there was a steady demand for them because I was still in the public eye. 'If only I could get hold of some I could sell them all day and make a fortune,' he moaned.

'Is that so?' I replied, and walked off feeling like a million dollars. It was a feeling I would have kept all day, but instead of leaving it at that I went back to him. 'Tell me,' I asked, 'this Screaming Lord Sutch bloke – why are his records so rare?'

'Because they never sold any in the first place,' he

replied scornfully, as though it was the most obvious thing in the world.

I didn't say anything, although the fact is my records have sold steadily over the years, even if only in small amounts, and some have never been deleted. But on that occasion I had spoiled things for myself by making the fatal error of asking the extra probing question. As I now informed Peter, I did not want us to make the same mistake. 'I think we should just leave things as they are and not investigate any further,' I told him.

'I agree,' he replied instantly, sighing with immense relief as he clambered off the mountain of plastic bags. 'You know, David, you may be a Loony, but that's the most sensible thing I've ever heard you say.'

So that's where I'll leave it – and really it makes no difference. For, all being well, I intend to stand in every possible election and by-election for the foreseeable future, representing the non-voters of Britain on the Official Monster Raving Loony thesis that if every smile was a vote we would win hands down every time.

The only thing that could prevent me from doing this would be you lot ballsing it up by actually voting me into Parliament.

But then, if you did, that would be the start of a whole new story.

EPILOGUE:
APRIL FOOLS, 1992

BEFORE THE General Election in April, I added to the various scalps on my belt by seeing off the Plaid Cymru candidate in the Monmouth by-election. But I already knew that in the General Election Britain's 'first past the post' voting system had been designed to ensure the Tory Party would stay in office for ever.

As this had cruelly robbed me of overall victory in advance I held urgent consultations at the bar of the Golden Lion in Ashburton and with my campaign manager Tony King up North. We decided on a new masterplan by which I would be the first party leader to leap ahead of the times and introduce proportional representation (PR) by standing against all three party leaders at once. This meant a lot of travelling round the country, as I also had more than twenty fellow Loony candidates to support – a record for the party and a tribute to their determination to be draft since they all had to stump up the required £500 deposit, despite the recession.

The Monster Raving Loony Party did unfortunately suffer one setback when our record, 'Number 10 or Bust', was banned from the airwaves during the campaign by the BBC. This was a blow despite the fact that I was used to this sort of censorship from my pirate radio days.

Instead I reverted to my preferred policy of live

music at various gigs. This started with the launch of our manifesto at Johnny O'Boogies' Rock and Roll Café near Leicester Square in Soho, kindly donated for the occasion by our Westminster candidate, Peter Stockton. Peter, whose chosen electoral gear consisted of a blue drape jacket, shimmering gold tie and black leather trousers, took me back to my mentor, Winston Churchill, in that his grandfather, Sir Edwin Stockton, had once defeated the great man at a general election during the 1920s.

Since he was in the constituency which contains the House of Commons, Peter was a great fan of our new policy of putting Parliament on wheels and sending it round the country. This was going to be Britain's answer to Disneyland, which was opened in France immediately after the election in tribute to all its candidates.

As my helicopter was unfortunately being serviced at the time, I toured the country in the Loony 'Strange Rover' reminding my candidates and the voters of the 'Three Rs' – reading, 'riting and rock and roll. But I knew that on the night even this valiant vehicle would not be enough to get me from Paddy Ashdown's seat in Yeovil to Islwyn, near Cardiff in Wales, where I was standing against Neil Kinnock, and then to Huntingdon for John Major.

So because I could not attend all three counts, and knowing he was going to win, I therefore chose Major's. This also gave me the chance to renew my acquaintance with my old friend Lord Buckethead of the Gremloids party, who was also standing there. When I arrived at the count I was told Major wanted to meet me, but I spent so long waiting, and was so exhausted by my campaigning, that I nodded off.

I awoke to see the new PM-to-be coming towards me, hand outstretched in greeting, and I hurriedly rose to shake it. I had some cause to thank Major, as his officials had previously agreed to let me into Downing Street for a look round and to measure up for curtains etc in preparation for the great day when I will move in. I know this is only a matter of time, but have decided to postpone my entry until the next century, when Britain will have gone further down the tube and voters will therefore have turned more to Loony ways of thinking.

I was given my tour of No. 10 early in the morning, when John and Norma were still asleep upstairs, and I now told him I hoped I had not woken him up. He assured me I had not and we then had a general chat, during which he told me he had admired me for years. I found myself unable to return the compliment as the effect of meeting him in the flesh was unfortunately sending me back to sleep again. It was only when Norma timidly asked me in her mousy little voice for some Loony money that I snapped back to life.

When the results were announced I found my 'Triple Crown' policy had been phenomenally successful, and a true tribute to how PR should work in this country. I had polled 728 votes against Major, 547 against Kinnock, and 338 against Ashdown. My vote against Major was also my highest ever. This did not, of course, surprise me in any way. It had been a long road from the days of Harold Wilson, but when I had examined John Major's grey suit at the count I had seen how very little things had changed. With the new dull note he had introduced to British politics I was not at all surprised voters were beginning to flock to the Loonies in droves, despite the appearance of the Natural Law Party with its appeal to those who float.

I also noted that Major had got the same point with his desperate appointment of David Mellor as the new 'Minister of Fun'. I could not help thinking that although David is incredibly lightweight the post might have been better filled by someone who really understands what fun is, such as myself.

As for the defeated Kinnock, I was able to console him by reminding him that it was not too late for him to revert to his previous career as a rock and roller. Unfortunately I fear he will never reach the dizzying heights in this field that I myself have attained. No doubt, long before the next election which will mark the next step in my steady climb to the top, he will be just another has-been.

I suppose that I should have felt sorry for him. But then, as Britain's longest-serving party leader, I have outlasted so many opponents that, to be perfectly honest, they soon turn into a blur. Funny, isn't it, how they make such a noise at the time and then disappear as if they have never been?

Only true Loonies, as we all know, go on for ever.

1992 Election Hall of Fame

Screaming Lord Sutch	Huntingdon	728
Screaming Lord Sutch	Islwyn	547
Screaming Lord Sutch	Yeovil	338
Alan 'Boss Hogg' Hope	Teignbridge	437
Baron Von Thunderclap	Sussex Mid	392
Sir Guy Francis	Blackpool	178
Russ Sharp	Stirling	68
Freddy Zapp	Falmouth and Cambourne	327
Wild Willy Beckett	Bradford North	350
T.C. Owen	Wokingham	531
Mel Hartshorne	Cannock and Burntwood	469
Chris Johnson	Chipping Barnet	213
'Boney Maroney'	Colne Valley	160
Lord Tiverton	Hastings and Rye	168
Stan Herley	Halton	398
Gerry Egan	Gower	114
Darren Poyzer	Stalybridge and Hyde	337
Adrian Wareham	Christchurch	175
Peter Stockton	City of London and Westminster	147
Maria Avino	Islington South and Finsbury	142
D. 'Newt' Beaupre	Kingston	212
Sally Ann Johnson	Finchley	130
Dino Martin	Antrim South	442
Nicky Winnington	Cambridge	175
'Dr Jekyll' Askwith	Windsor and Maidenhead	236
David Langstaff	Workington	755
'Dangerous Dave' Rea	Spelthorne	338